FIRST STAGE

First Stage

THE MAKING OF THE STRATFORD FESTIVAL

TOM PATTERSON
and
Allan Gould

McClelland and Stewart

Canadian Cataloguing in Publication Data

Patterson, Tom, 1920–
First stage

ISBN 0-7710-6949-9

1. Stratford Festival (Ont.) – History.
2. Theatre – Canada – History. 3. Patterson,
Tom, 1920–   . I. Gould, Allan, 1944–
II. Title.

PN2306.S72S7 1987   792'.09713'23   C87-093300-0

McClelland and Stewart
The Canadian Publishers
481 University Avenue
Toronto, Ontario
M5G 2E9

Printed and bound in Canada by John Deyell Co.

TO PAT

who wanted to be in Stratford in 1953,
and to the citizens of Stratford,
without whom none of this
would have happened.

Contents

Preface

Even after thirty-five years, it still amazes me how the Stratford Festival came together in such a short time – less than two years. In comparison, think of the roughly fifty years it took to get a National Theatre in England; of the nearly a decade of planning and the money spent to replace Toronto's Massey Hall with the Roy Thompson Hall; how, even in hustling New York City, it took many years and millions of dollars (not to mention many scathing arguments and resulting animosities) to build the Lincoln Center. Our Festival went from empty talk to performance in less than two years!

How, then, did our "miracle" happen?

Basically, there were four groups without whom the Festival could not have been created – and, incidentally, without whom I would have had to go back to writing about sewage plants for *Civic Administration* magazine!

The first group, of course, were the professionals – Tony Guthrie, Tanya Moiseiwitsch, Cecil Clarke and his wife Jacqueline Cundall, Ray Diffen and Annette Geber, and other giants of modern theatre, who will be given their due in the following pages. Without their unselfishness and sacrifice, and their ever-ready offers of help, it would have been impossible to engender the enthusiasm that kept the rest of us going.

Then there was the Stratford board. A group of Stratford business and professional men, together with a few homemakers, who, at the onset, could not in the largest stretch of the imagination have been called "theatre buffs." But they did have solid, conservative backgrounds and, as Tony Guthrie noted in a letter to Alec Guinness, "were unsophisticated, but one must not confuse unsophistication with unintelligence."

There were also many volunteer committees and individuals who, I must admit, sometimes created more problems than they solved, but who, nevertheless, had very large hearts for the most part in the right places.

Last, but not least, there was the administrative staff: Mary Joliffe, who was our publicist extraordinaire. She came on board sometime in November 1952, and made all the difference in the world.

There was Florence Pelton, who left her job as switchboard operator and secretary at the Whyte Packing Co., a meat packing plant started by my great-grandfather, to become my secretary.

Fran Tompkins, the wife of a Stratford alderman became one of us, first as a part-time worker and eventually full-time, later that eventful spring.

And although he was not part of the administrative staff I must mention Cecil Clarke here, as well.

Each of these extraordinary individuals will get some of their due (it could never, ever be sufficient!) in the pages that follow. But what happened to each? Mary Joliffe stayed with us through the first crucial years, and then went on to do wondrous work at the O'Keefe Centre, the National Ballet of Canada, the Guthrie Theater in Minneapolis, the Metropolitan Opera, the Canada Council, and, today, as Communications Director for the Ontario Arts Council.

Florence Pelton, born on a farm near Embro, a village not far from Stratford, eventually married my brother, worked her marvels for many years with the Festival, and recently retired in 1984.

Fran Tompkins went on to become a continuing stalwart to the Festival Board of Governors, as the Foundation Secretary.

There were others, of course: Vera Mackenzie, originally from Office Overload, who worked in our Toronto office that first summer and became a mainstay; and Doug Henderson, a young man who had read something about the upcoming Festival in the papers, walked into our office to see if he could help, and did, thousands of times, over those tense, difficult few months. And in between the ever-increasing meetings, members of the Stratford board continually contributed their services.

But, essentially, it was this group of five which held things together – co-ordinating with the board, doing press relations, campaigning, contacting the company of performers, organizing the accommodations, and dealing with the hundreds of other unexpected problems which arose from day to day.

The amazing thing is that, in spite of all the stress and strain – and there was plenty, as you will soon read – I cannot recall a single harsh word ever being spoken between us. It was probably because of our good senses of humour. Indeed, I can't remember any period of time in my life when I have laughed as much. I think it was that laughter that got us through.

Thanks must also go to two unsung heroes of the Festival: Evelyn Brownell and Monty Monteith. Evelyn was with the Ontario Department of Industry and was a good friend of the Hon. Dana Porter, the number-two man in the Ontario government at the time. It was Evelyn who smoothed my path in dealing with government agencies. Monty, a Stratford business man and politician, was influential in engineering the crucial $25,000 grant that made the Festival possible.

Thanks are in order too, regarding this book, to theatrical agent Madrienne McKeown, who introduced me to Vancouver film-maker Jack Darcus, in 1984. It was he, after hearing several stories about how the Festival started, who said the usual thing: "You should write a book!" I had heard this refrain many times before, but was surprised when, the next day, Jack declared, "Come on – we're going to buy a tape recorder and I'm going to get all this down." With no thought of pecuniary reward – thank heavens he had been visiting Toronto from Vancouver – he sat me down, many afternoons in a row, in the Hop & Grape pub in Toronto, and we talked for nearly two-dozen hours. It is from these tapes, transcribed by my daughter Lucy, and Linda Lord, now a student at the National Theatre School, that the bulk of this story has arisen.

Also, thanks to Herb Whittaker, not only for his encouragement, but his invaluable help – through his early reporting as well as in providing much detailed information for this book; to Barb Reid, who did not come to the Festival until after the first year, but who is a mine of information about the early days.

Thanks, too, to the Stratford Festival Archives, as well as the Public Archives of Canada in Ottawa, for supplying both information and pictures; the Stratford *Beacon Herald* for their photographs and also, most importantly, for access to their files.

Financially, this book could not have been possible without the help of Dr. Nick Laidlaw of the Laidlaw Foundation, and the Ontario Arts Council, which has been so supportive.

I must also thank my agent, Pat Stewart, without whose enthusiasm and knowledge I doubt this work could have come to fruition.

The co-author of *First Stage*, Allan Gould, not only managed to put all this thirty-five-year-old information together in an organized manner, but did it with great theatrical knowledge (his university doctoral thesis was on the theatre criticism of Toronto drama critic Nathan Cohen), and great humour.

To Dinah Forbes, my editor, the greatest thanks. She not only provided keen intelligence but also knowledge of the theatre, being born in Stratford-upon-Avon, England. She and Allan both expressed that sense of fun that a third of a century ago made the Festival possible.

None of this, though, could have happened without the enthusiasm and support of publisher Jack McClelland. His belief in Canada and in telling Canadians about their own country is well known. All Canadians should be grateful to him.

Finally, to all those unsung heroes in Stratford who, by their individual and joint efforts, assured the success of the Festival, my heartfelt appreciation. I am sorry that it is impossible to name them all, but I do want to thank them.

Tom Patterson,
February, 1987.

1

A Little Backwoods Hamlet

"Public opinion, insofar as it has as yet been plumbed, seems favorable – and it ought to be said at this point that it will require hard work, zealous team-work, and generous financial support if the venture is to succeed. In a word, it behooves all concerned – organizations and individual citizens alike – to get a realistic perspective of the size of the financial problem involved. For it is self-evident that unless the Festival and associated enterprises are on a scale that will attract patronage from far and near, it cannot achieve the exalted goal which Mr. Patterson has in mind."

Editorial,
The Beacon-Herald,
January 1952

"Let us establish this Shakespeare theatre and festival by all means (and entirely at our expense) – but let's have it in Toronto. Toronto people, I understand, have been mad about the project from the start. They'd be broken-hearted, I fear, if we did not go through with it. (Of course, it would be no skin off their pretty noses if we went flat on ours.) . . .

"Well then, set up this theatre in Toronto. You couldn't expect those Toronto fans to come up here for the performances any more than for the parties. We'd have to pay the fare for enthusiasts from the United States, too, of course, for the same reason. Stratford people could pay their own way down – we're the ones that hatched this thing, anyway, because every one of us has been itching for years to revive the real Shakespeare, and it's only right that we should pay, and pay plenty. Another nice thing about having it in Toronto would be that the audience would have all of Lake Ontario to flop into after sitting out a Shakespeare play in a tent in one of our Summers."

> Letter to the editor,
> *The Beacon-Herald*,
> July 1952.

These two excerpts from the Stratford, Ontario, newspaper in 1952 – the former, from when the Festival was barely a glimmer in the eyes of the Stratford City Council; the latter, from the week that Tyrone Guthrie first visited Canada – capture the two prevailing views of the time. The astonishing fact that the Stratford Festival had its opening night on July 13, 1953, almost one year to the day after Tony Guthrie first set foot in our small town, suggests that the sympathetic editorial was far more indicative of the eventual attitudes of Canadians – and men and women around the world – than the sarcastic letter to the editor.

What sort of men and women would provide that "hard work, zealous team-work, and generous financial support" which *The Beacon-Herald* correctly identified as the necessary ingredients for an internationally respected Festival, planning its thirty-fifth year as I write?

The answer was not clearly apparent in 1952. As a writer in the *Toronto Telegram* noted at the time, Stratford-upon-Avon, England, may have been synonymous with Shakespeare, but Stratford, Ontario, was synonymous with hockey. In our namesake in the Old Country, boards were *trod upon* by performers; in Canada's Stratford, they were something to be *knocked into*. It seemed as if there was a Stratford native on every team of the National Hockey League: George Armstrong, Joffre Desilets, Ray Getliffe, Joe Klukay, Al Murray. Older hockey fans could rattle off an earlier generation: Dolly Dolson, George Hay, Wally Hearn, Harold Hicks, Toots

Holway, and, of course, the renowned "Stratford Streak," Howie Morenz.

To go from a town that hollered hockey to one that shouted Shakespeare was not an easy feat, but there have been many clues to the remarkable nature of Stratford's citizens over the past century and a half.

After the war of 1812, the British government granted a million acres of land along Lake Huron to the Canada Company, which was headed by a Scottish businessman (and poet), John Galt. We call such men pioneers, but in truth they were developers. They took what was called Huron Tract, and, according to the conditions of the agreement with England, they had to build an inn and a church, roughly every fourteen miles. (This distance was approximately one day's walk through the bush.) Indeed, if you travel from Guelph to Goderich today, you encounter another town around fourteen miles after the last.

While hacking a road to Lake Huron, the surveyors came to a marshy creek surrounded by a thick forest, named it Little Thames, and noted what they described as "a good mill-site." Galt's less-renowed replacement, Thomas Mercer Jones, named the area Stratford, which means, purportedly, a narrow crossing. The year was 1832, exactly 150 years before the concept of a Stratford Festival truly took hold.

In one of those name-dropping, prosaic books of the turn of the century (*History of the County of Perth From 1825 to 1902* by William Johnston), one can read of the extremely inauspicious beginnings of the town: "In all new commercial centres material progress at the outset is accelerated or retarded by their environment having a natural adaptability for agricultural purposes. There was no town in Perth Country, nor, indeed, in the Huron Tract, located in a spot so destitute in its surroundings of those elements which give life to a backwoods hamlet."

"Backwoods" was not half of it. Quoting a visitor to Stratford in 1852, who described the village as one which "did not partake of a cheerful character," Johnston wrote, somewhat drolly, that "a little backwoods hamlet in the centre of a swamp, where, about seven years prior to the period [1852], a settler had wandered from his home, and was devoured by wolves within what is now the city limits, was not likely to be very cheerful." "Exit, pursued by bear," the famous Shakespearean stage direction from *A Winter's Tale*, would have to wait a bit longer before it would be experienced within the Stratford city limits.

Jones, the man who gave Stratford its name, eventually renamed the Little Thames "the Avon," and donated an oil painting of William Shakespeare to the first settlers of the village, who tacked it up on the outside of the first building, the Shakespeare Inn. It is rumoured that the village changed its name as well, to Stratford-on-Avon, but post office officials found that a bit wordy, if not presumptuous, and kept slashing off the "on-Avon" until the longer name was eventually dropped.

Stratford may have the highest elevation of any town in the province of Ontario – 1,150 feet above sea level – but it was too swampy in its earliest few decades to grow very rapidly. Then, in 1871, what was fondly known as "Muddy Stratford" was made a division point for the Grand Trunk Railway, which soon made it far more attractive to industry and population.

By the turn of the century, Stratford had another major industry to join the railroad: furniture. But the muddy, ugly, stump-filled Avon was the shame of the town, bordered by a livery stable, a junk yard, a bottle-strewn ashery, and – as hard as it is to believe today – the city dump.

The saviour of Stratford's Avon was Tom Orr, an insurance broker who was appointed secretary to the new Parks Board in 1904. Four years earlier, the Ontario Park Act provided one half-mill of the city assessment for parks, and Orr found himself with a golden opportunity to turn a cesspool into a dream.

At that time, Stratford had one small park on the Avon at its eastern limit, and another, Queen Victoria Park, at its western limit. Orr's vision was as complex as it was obvious;

he wished to join the two parks at each end of the city and make the entire riverfront into one large park.

The Parks Board thought he was crazy, but he went ahead and hired an Ottawa landscape architect (for fifty dollars, plus expenses) to come to Stratford and draw up a plan. Interestingly, the architect he hired was the same man who designed the parks for the Rideau Canal system in Ottawa, as I recall, so he was no slouch. His drawings were accepted, but no one knew where to obtain the money necessary to purchase all the land involved. (Clearly I was not the first Tom to encounter difficult circumstances in making an ambitious idea come to fruition in Stratford, Ontario.)

Tom Orr proceeded to turn Stratford's riverfront into a garden. He persuaded the City Council to issue debentures in the amount of $10,000 to a dam syndicate that owned most of the property adjoining the Avon in the eastern half of the city (after proving that the sale of ice and water-power rights would carry the payments.) He cleaned out the creek and dredged it for boating. He fought off a new clothing factory, which wanted to build on the banks of the Avon and which offered jobs and increased taxes to the city, by taking out the option on the property himself and persuading the enraged Stratford Board of Trade that the factory would ruin the park.

Then, in 1912, Orr fought his greatest battle. Canadian Pacific Railway attempted to run a line through the park, build a station smack in the middle, and drop freight sheds on land already set aside for tennis courts. Five of the seven men on the Parks Board agreed with the mayor, who felt, along with twelve of the fourteen aldermen, that the city could well use a second railway, the increased property values, additional industry, and lower freight rates. Tom Orr's response was inspired. He rushed the building of a boathouse on the shore of the Avon, so the citizens, who were soon to have a public vote on the railway, would be able to see with their own eyes from mid-river how the trains would ruin their new park system. He stood on the post office corner, pleaded with passersby, drew maps and charts to make his point, and even wrote letters to out-of-town citizens, right across Canada, begging them to come home and vote for

Beauty. The CPR, not to be outdone, offered free tickets to property owners across the country, to come home and vote for Progress. The final tally was a slim majority of eighty-six votes in favour of the park and against the railway (and Progress).

Even more relevant to my story was Tom Orr's visit to England between the wars, where he spent much of his time in Stratford-upon-Avon. He studied the gardens surrounding the properties there and resolved that his beloved park should have the same. The perfect place was just west of the bridge and behind the courthouse, where the well-established firm of E.T. Dufton Woollen Mills was situated.

This time, Orr did not have to fight for his plan. A fire destroyed the mills (no, there is no proof that Orr was behind the deed), and Orr talked the City Council into offering $10,000 for the site. The owners countered with $16,000; Orr claimed that he "could wait." The Parks Board eventually obtained the property for $7,000. Today, every flower mentioned in the plays of Shakespeare – monkshood to sneeze worse, bee balm to bachelor's button – blooms in Orr's formal English garden.

Lest this be thought to be all based on historical sources, I should inform the reader that I used to date Tom Orr's daughter, Peggy, and often visited her at their home, which was but four or five blocks away from my own. As a child I was aware of Tom Orr's importance to Stratford, but, I must confess, we pretty much took the beautiful park system for granted back then, not unlike the way most Stratfordians probably take the Festival for granted today.

Tom told me about one incident that took place before the war. As he was an insurance man, Tom knew much about the construction of Stratford's buildings. One factory, which was made of handsome St. Mary's stone, had closed because of the Depression. Orr quickly made a deal with the wreckers. He persuaded them, rather than dump the debris outside the town, to leave it by the river. Then Orr made another deal, this one with the city. He requested that they send down itinerent labourers to work the stone. In this way he ended up obtaining free labour to build stone walls and embankments around his beloved Shakespearean garden.

Tom Orr was nearly stone deaf and wore a hearing aid, which he used almost as creatively as he used the parks system. He would order his workers, "Don't put it *there* for heaven's sake! Put it *there!*" And then he would turn off his hearing aid. "Tom," he explained, "I do that so they can let off steam and swear at me without me hearing it. This way, I don't have to get mad at them!"

Tom Orr did not always get his way, however, although he was certainly more prescient than most human beings. There was a jail, some three-hundred yards beyond the gardens. Orr once told me, when I was a teenager, "One day, that jail over there will be gone, and the garden will sweep all the way up to the high school! And we'll change the face of the school, so that it will look upon the park." Well, the jail is still there, a half-century after Tom Orr shared one of his many dreams with me.

In case the above tales of Tom Orr's admirable work on behalf of Stratford's park system make him appear like an aesthetic Jesus, creating the rock/garden upon which I would build my church/theatre, let me quote from an interview with the old man, then in his early eighties, in the summer of 1952. "Why would we want ten thousand people tramping around on our grass? This park was built for the people of Stratford." So much for agreement amongst pioneers.

It is difficult to overestimate and overpraise the extraordinary work of Tom Orr. It was Orr, more than anyone else, who helped me realize that one can, indeed, make things happen. He taught me that one cannot just sit around hoping and waiting. When a member of the citizen's committee was asked to write Tyrone Guthrie, in late spring 1952, to give the director a sense of the facilities Stratford had to offer as a festival site, he was unsure of what to declare. Then he compared an aerial photograph of our city's park with a photo of the park in Stratford-upon-Avon, England. The two were nearly identical.

There have been, then, many examples of passion and drive in Stratford's history. It has been a community which has' repeatedly shown itself to be willing to sacrifice financial gain in favour of what its citizens thought was "right." Choosing Tom Orr's park over a revenue-producing railway is a half-century-old example. Yet as recently as 1951, shortly before the concept of a Shakespearean Festival caught fire, Stratford's Industrial Commission turned down a plan of General Electric to build a plant that would have employed one thousand people. The president of the Commission at the time defended its decision in a particularly Stratford-like fashion: "What's the point of crowding our schools, our housing, all our city services? We make the town a worse place to live in, and what good does it do us?. . .We want growth, but we want sound growth. Size doesn't mean anything in itself."

This small-town sensibility – that progress is *not* measured in dollars, population, or numbers of factories – is why Stratford gained but 1,043 people between the 1931 and 1951 censuses, while nearby Guelph and Kitchener doubled their respective populations. It is the same sensibility which allowed me to dream, and dream in colour, about a world-class Shakespearean Festival.

My own past goes deep into the rich soil of Stratford, Ontario, although, for some reason, many writers have thought otherwise. I still cannot fathom why such an excellent journalist as Alexander Ross (in *The Booming Fifties*, in the *Canada's Illustrated Heritage* series) would write "Stratford . . .started as a crazy idea in the head of an English immigrant named Tom Patterson."

This rather unconventional English immigrant was born in 1920 in Stratford, the fourth child of Harry Murray Patterson and his wife, Lucinda Whyte Patterson. The first of my family to come to Canada was also a Tom, born in the late 1820s in Edinburgh. As a young man in Scotland, my ancestor and namesake was apprenticed to a firm of mechanics who built and maintained the new steam engines which were spreading across Great Britain during that period. (The first railway in the world opened in Yorkshire in 1813; the first one built in Scotland was seen by my great-great-grandfather, as a child).

When the Grand Trunk Railway planned to construct a major workshop in Stratford, Ontario, to service the trains that ran up to Port Huron, Michigan, across the river from Sarnia, they sent their London, Ontario, agent to Scotland to recruit skilled men. Among the recruits was Thomas Patterson, aged forty, who brought members of two Patterson families with him. They all worked at the Grand Trunk steam-engine repair shops. The last Patterson to work in these shops was my father, Harry Patterson, born in Stratford in 1885, who followed his predecessors into the "family business." He became a skilled mechanic, but as the railway was by then part of the Canadian National system, his sense of enterprise was frustrated by his being an employee of a gigantic company. He eventually left CN and set up his own business when the Grand Trunk went on strike in 1905. My father said "the hell with it," quit, and borrowed enough money from his father-in-law to start Patterson's Book Store, which remained under that name until 1960. He was never a great reader of books, but he was a good salesman. So he would get my mother to read them and tell him the story lines, which he would repeat to his customers as if he knew what he was talking about. In 1927, he left the literary world to become plant manager of the Stratford Brass Company, eventually becoming its president, and where he remained until his death in 1942.

It would be lovely to claim that my father's bookstore was a profound influence on my later interest in creating a Shakespearean Festival, but it is simply not so. Indeed, I do not even recall ever hearing my mother telling the plots to my father. It was only many years later that she told me of it.

My father never graduated from anything after public school, yet he was perennially elected to the Stratford Board of Education, and many times he topped the polls. It was great fun for my siblings and myself when the local band – a group of Stratford musicians – came around to our house on election night and serenaded his victory. This made a great impression on me, and I vowed back then that I would work to merit someday the same kind of attention my dad was receiving. I did not realize until many years later that the main reason why the band performed for him was to get the free drinks he provided.

My mother, Lucinda Whyte Patterson, was also of Scottish

descent, with some English thrown in, making my "English immigrant" status all the more remarkable. John Whyte, the first of the family to come to Canada, was born at Loch Lomond in 1822 and was apprenticed as a young man to a stone mason in Glasgow, where he married Margaret Miller, in 1848.

The young couple sought their fortunes in the New World that same year. Whyte worked on the construction of the Erie Railroad in New York, on the Old City Hall of Hamilton, the old Court House at Chatham, and on both the Court House and stone bridge at Stratford. Quite the entrepreneur, Whyte bought land for a farm in Hibbert Township, near Stratford. He cleared the forest, cultivated the land, built a house and barns. By 1873, with a flourishing farm, he began a new business, that of meat-packing. The plant thrived, and three of his sons took over the family firm. The eldest, John Whyte Jr., born in 1850 in Mitchell, Ontario, became manager.

He moved the business to Stratford in 1900, taking with him his wife and family, including a daughter, Lucinda, who had been born in 1887. In 1909, she married my father, Harry Murray Patterson, making my brothers, my sister, and myself the fourth generation of Whytes and Pattersons in Canada.

As far back as I can remember, my family supported me, or rather, they never stood in the way of any madcap scheme that I wanted to do. At the age of twelve, I went to the local YMCA camp for two weeks during the summer. But instead of coming home with the drivers, another fellow and I decided to hitchhike home. It was haying time on the farms, and as we waited for a car to pick us up on the Blue Water Highway, a young, red-headed farmer, not much older than I, leaned over his fence and asked us if we wanted a job. I told him that I had to go home first, but that I would be back that Monday morning. I knew full well that my parents would encourage me.

An even better example of my future success as an impresario, for want of a better word, is what happened when I was in my mid-teens. One of my school assignments was the obligatory "oral composition." Most of the subjects chosen by the other students were on the line of "How I spent my summer holidays" – classically boring subjects. But since the Great Depression was still very much with us (this was around 1936) I was familiar with how the unemployed used to go from town to town, using the local jail as their "hotel." I decided that for my assignment I wanted to speak about the Depression and its effect on our society.

For a teenaged boy, I was quite sensitive to the despair of the times. I remember unemployed men traipsing into our kitchen frequently during those difficult years, where my mother would give them free meals, although, if they looked too scruffy, they never got past the back porch! This may have been as often as three, even four times each week. It was rumoured in those days that many houses were "marked"; that is, the travelling fellows somehow knew who were the "good folk" who would provide them with food. I would look out the window and see the destitute walk past a number of houses, fresh from the trains they had hopped across Canada, and then stop, consciously and deliberately, at ours.

I quickly got permission from my father and then made arrangements with the local chief of police to lock me up, every night for a week, to interview these knights of the road. I also went to the parks where the men would sleep, using newspapers as blankets, and spoke with dozens of them. Many of my parents' friends thought that they were insane to allow their son to do this, but both my mother and father thought that it was a marvellous experience for me, and were thrilled when my speech, entitled "Tramps, Hobos, and Bums," received a 99 per cent mark. (The head of the English department, Miss Rose McQueen, later admitted to a fellow teacher that she had wanted to give Tom Patterson's composition 100 per cent, but she had assumed that there had to have been something wrong with it, so she had taken off one mark. The Canadian inferiority complex, Stratford version!)

Earlier in that same decade, Stratford was the site of one of the biggest Depression strikes in Canada. The city was chosen, I believe, because it was an industrial city with a large furniture industry as well as such firms as the Swift packing company. It was very easy in those days for organizers to tie up a small town. So, although the actual number of strikers was not great (if they had been on strike in Toronto, it would have not shown much) the struggle split the town in two, closing it down.

Stratford soon acquired an awful reputation, including that of being the Communist headquarters for Canada. It is difficult to believe it today, but the City Council used to open their meetings with a singing of "The Internationale." The Presbyterian Minister, the Rev. Dr. Duncan – a man with a bush of white hair and white mustache – understandably, and ferociously, tried to drown out the dangerous, subversive tune with his own, solo version of "God Save the King."

Finally, the premier of Ontario at the time, Mitch Hepburn, sent in the troops. The men, from the Royal Canadian Regiment, the RCR, one of the few permanent regiments in our part of the country, moved in with what we, as children, called tanks. They were actually some sort of machine-gun carriers, but they looked quite ferocious to us at the time.

There was fighting in the streets. At Swift Packing, the troops tried to put a truck through the barbed wire surrounding the plant, and the strikers attacked it and turned it over. It was filled with butter, and this was a very hot day. The workers picked up soft pounds of butter and heaved them at the photographers. It was great fun for all the children, including me, who were sitting there, but it created a disastrous reputation for Stratford, from a labour point of view. It was clear that no new industry would want to locate in our town for the foreseeable future.

Some half-dozen years later, in 1939, I was running a booth in a gas station owned by a man named Ken Wright, whose father had been a striker, back in that fateful year in Stratford history. One day, Ken approached me and declared, "My dad wants me to tell you to thank your dad for what he did during the strike." During that period my father ran a factory that was not on strike, and I still like to believe that he had something to do with settling the dreadful dispute.

This awful period has since provided the occasional, quite charming anecdote. One of the organizers was a man named Isadore Minster, who looked quite a bit like Stalin and even smoked a pipe like the Soviet dictator. Several years later, when the Stratford Festival had begun, a man came into the office of the Festival's manager, Vic Polley, to apologize because he had backed into a car in our parking lot. Vic took the details down, and the man was embarrassed to admit that he was none other than Isadore Minster, one-time strike leader, who had come back to Stratford to sell wax to coat and treat the wood of our Festival stage. How the mighty socialists had become capitalists, just two decades later.

I have no doubt that the Stratford Strike had a social impact on me, if nothing else, as a lot of my friends at that time were the children of strikers. My friends and I knew one thing for sure: We wanted to graduate from high school and get the hell out of Stratford. We spoke a great deal about going to such larger cities as Kitchener or London. The Big Dream, of course, was to go to Toronto. There was no living to be made in Stratford. So instead of going out and searching for work, and because we lacked the money to go to university, we went back and repeated our fifth year in high school, now Grade 13. It is a sad comment on that era that we were happy to take the same year twice (with a few extra subjects we liked), just to spend the time in a warm place.

We would sit in class, and if we didn't like the one that followed, we would go outside and kibitz. The teacher, Rose McQueen, knew that we were good, thoughtful kids, so she did not mind. (She lived to see the Festival, by the way, and was very proud of me! Once, in 1953, before the Festival opened, and we were running out of money, there was a fateful meeting which she attended. My former teacher did not think that we could go on, when she looked at the situation objectively. She told me later, "I think that it is a lost cause, since you have no money, but I didn't want to vote against you, Tom. So I got up and left the meeting when it came to a vote.")

The courthouse was just down the street from our school, so I and a few buddies used to sit in on court cases. (Stratford is the county seat of Perth, so a lot happened in our courthouse.) Then we would go down and relax on the grassy bank behind our school, overlooking the beautiful Avon River.

We were all boys, maybe three or four of us. The war

scattered most of us, but I still remember Jim McCardle, who
ended up quite high in External Affairs in Ottawa and who
was eventually made Ambassador to Ireland, and Mick
Graham, who stayed in Stratford, and who I still see the
odd time. We would sit on the banks of the Avon and argue
about our school football team, which was invariably beaten
by the team from Woodstock, Ontario. (That we could never
beat Woodstock was the bane of every kid in Stratford. It
was a smaller town, too!)

We also used to discuss what was going to happen to
Stratford, which we felt was dying. It was still a CN town,
back in the late 1930s, and we all knew that the diesel was
coming in. We understood it would be only a matter of time
until the giant steam-engine repair shops, which my father,
grandfather, and great-grandfather once worked in, and on
which the town depended, would be put to rest.

The other fellows and I used to think up ways of trying
to save our native town. One idea had to do, not surprisingly,
with hockey. We had an artificial ice-rink, so we dreamed
of an international hockey school in the summertime. I did
not like hockey very much; my feet got too cold. So the
idea of a hockey school failed to thrill me. The concept did
not stick with the other guys for very long, although a hockey
school was eventually set up in Stratford, sometime in the
1960s, using some players from the National Hockey League.
It lasted only a few years.

Another idea, my own, was to create a Shakespearean
Festival. After all, I argued, we had a city named Stratford,
on a river named Avon. We had a beautiful park system.
We had wards and schools with such names as Hamlet,
Falstaff, Romeo, and Juliet. We even had a bronze head of
the great dramatist by the Canadian sculptor Cleeve Horne,
which had been donated to the city by the Sons of England.

Why not a Festival? And, what better place than in
Stratford, Ontario?

My original idea was to have the prospective Festival in
the open air. The picture I had in my mind was not of a
building, nor of a stage, as I knew absolutely nothing about
theatre, or of how it worked. Rather I had an image only

of lots of people pouring in, and this began to develop in my mind.

Like a fanciful child, who pictures faces and figures in the clouds, I gazed at the empty park and saw the crowds already gathered. My idea was to stage the play in the park's shell band stand and to seat the audience on the surrounding slope. After all, thanks to Tom Orr, there were plenty of park benches there. All I would have to do was cut off the road, River Drive, which runs in front of the band shell.

Most theatres, of course, are started by actors or directors – in other words, by theatre people, whose total concern is for what will go on the stage. But because I did not know what was involved in producing a play, I was able to concentrate, in my teenaged mind, on getting the people there to see what might happen on stage.

I never had a vision of Ye Olde Festivale, or anything coy like that; I was very practical. "We don't *have* to build a building," I told my buddies, "and the space is available from the Parks Board."

It was a practical, childlike, even childish vision of theatre. And, just as sometimes happens to children's wishes, it would come true.

2

The Bare Beginnings

I n 1939, immediately after World War II began, I tried to join the Perth Regiment. But, at that early stage in the hostilities, the recruiters were very choosy. Anyone with glasses was immediately ruled out, and I had worn glasses since the age of seventeen. So the last year of that decade found me running a hot-dog stand in one of the local gas stations where one of my regular customers was a dentist, Dr. Bill Hamilton.

On one of his late-night visits to my place of business he announced that he had just joined the Canadian Dental Corps, and he invited me to be his dental assistant. Within a few days, I again took the recruiters' test. This time, they found that I had a hernia, which led to a spell in hospital. Two weeks after I got out, I was finally accepted as a soldier.

I left Halifax for England on June 11, 1940 – my twentieth birthday – and spent the war going through Great Britain, Normandy, on through France into Belgium, Holland, and Germany, before returning to Halifax five years less a day later.

In the Dental Corps, we were attached to a regiment only for a short time before moving to the next. This arrangement suited Dr. Hamilton and myself to a tee. One of our bosses, the colonel of the Dental Corps, was always at Headquarters, and the other boss, the regimental colonel, was only ever temporarily in command. This meant, in practice, that we had no bosses, as we played each man against the other and made our own arrangements. In retrospect, this freedom to act probably served me in good stead when I began to work on the Stratford Festival.

Even during the war, I never gave up my dream. I remember talking with friends I had made in England. "What are you going to do when you get home, after the war?" I was once asked. "I'm going to start a Shakespearean Festival in my home town," was my prompt reply.

I was never "a good soldier," in the military sense, but because of the liberty I had, I found time to make friends in each country I was in. One of my favourite memories from this period was when I was hitchhiking back to camp after a late night out. I practically forced my way into the back seat of a car and was stunned to discover that the driver and passenger were Sir Anthony Eden and his wife. We had a great conversation, and he talked fairly freely as I did not let on that I knew who he was. Unfortunately, I had to tell him where I wanted to go before I realized his identity; otherwise, I would have happily gone AWOL and travelled right to London with him.

Later, in Holland, at the tip of the Nijmegen salient, another incident took place, one which would affect my life back in Canada. I was billeted in the home of a Jew, who had been hidden all through the war by his very brave wife, a gentile. We became close friends, and through them I became involved with the Gelderland Province Underground. After the war, I started an import and export business, dealing with these same people of the Dutch Underground. The enterprise proved to be abortive, mainly because of my ignorance of business, as well as the fact that our first shipment of goods was broken into and most of it stolen. Perhaps it was for the best – my lack of entrepreneurship allowed me more time to work on my crazy teenage dream of creating a Shakespearean Festival for my home town.

This is the place to confess that, as a youth in Canada, I had never been to a live professional performance. (In various places, the great director Tyrone Guthrie has written that "Tom Patterson had seen opera in Italy," but he was, alas, quite mistaken. Indeed, I never even made it to Italy until many years after the Stratford Festival was established.) True, I had performed in a school production of what I believe was *Pirates of Penzance*, and I made a great contribution: I had to hang a lamp on a curtain, and the damn thing fell off and broke in the middle of the performance.

The first, live professional performance I saw was in London during the war. We received free tickets from the Canadian soldier's Beaver Club in London to see Vic Oliver in a revue. Soldiers traditionally were given front-row seats, so it was not terribly surprising that I was called up onto the stage, where I made my "professional" debut, dancing on the stage in a Vic Oliver revue.

It was the biggest moment of my life (up to that point). I ended up dancing with a woman in her sixties or seventies. I was quite proud of myself. She was a great dancer, and we had a ball. To be on the same stage as a vintage performer like Vic Oliver was quite the thrill for a lad in his early twenties from small-town Canada But with that one rather wild exception – and hardly a "legitimate" theatrical exception – I saw absolutely no other live theatre in my youth, other than the troop shows that occasionally came around to perform for the soldiers.

I remember being warned, probably for reasons of jealousy, that I should never visit Stratford-upon-Avon, England. It would spoil me, I was told. The British city was not nearly as beautiful as my native town, and it was a tourist trap, with a theatre that (reportedly) looked like a barn. The man who warned me was a Stratford fellow, David Holmes, who had the nickname of "Cocky," back in our town. He had gone overseas before I did, and I first encountered him there just a few weeks after I had arrived. I began to talk about my Festival concept, to which he responded with his warning not to visit Stratford-upon-Avon's "ugly" theatre. "Cocky" ended up as a school teacher, and an active civic person in Goderich, a town some forty-five miles from Stratford. In later years, he visited the Festival, and congratulated me on its creation. But it was because of him I never visited England's Stratford while I was there and I was "Over There" for more than four years.

I did not visit Stratford-upon-Avon until the fall of 1952, when I first met, and hired, the brilliant designer Tanya Moiseiwitsch. But the theatre did not upset me, even though it presents its side to you as you approach it from the town and could easily be mistaken for a biscuit factory. During that visit, I was too excited to be in Wardrobe with the glorious Tanya Moiseiwitsch to be critical.

After I arrived back in Halifax on the day before my twenty-fifth birthday, I returned to Stratford, Ontario. My sister-in-law was living at our home, because my older brother, Robert Whyte Patterson, had been killed in action with the Perth Regiment in Italy, a few days before Christmas 1944.

The young widow was in a play-reading group in Stratford, and in an attempt to get me back into the swing of things in the city, she invited me to sit in on its meetings. The group consisted of perhaps seven or eight men and women in their thirties and forties, most of them non-native Stratfordians, who had come to our town to work for the Children's Aid Society, where my sister-in-law was also employed. They would read works by such authors as Bernard Shaw, often aloud, and then discuss them.

At one of these gatherings during the summer of 1945, I brought up my eight-year-old idea of a Shakespearean Festival for Stratford. Everyone in the play-reading group thought it was a fine concept, so we began to write letters to people in power. (Since they were not "established" Stratfordians, none of these men and women ended up on the Festival committee, although I admit there would be a sense of romantic justice if some of them had.) I recall writing to no less a cultural bigwig than Sir Ernest MacMillan, the conductor of the Toronto Symphony Orchestra, and I know that we received one of the last letters that Lord Bennett ever wrote, since it arrived shortly before his death.

At this point, however, the Festival was hardly the magnificent obsession it came to be. It was nothing more than a nice idea, and because it was being discussed in a play-reading group, it seemed like a natural thing as well. The four or five letters we received all said essentially the same thing: "This sounds like a great idea." And that was all. I went to the mayor of Stratford at the time, Maurice King, and admitted that "we need a little bit of money now" for the concept. His reply was to the effect, "Oh, sure. We'll support you on that."

This rather casual meeting was in the United Cigar Store in Stratford, on the corners of Ontario and Downie Streets, at ten in the morning, the usual coffee break in the town. Then Mayor King asked me directly, "How much do you want?"

"Well. . .I don't know, you know," I stammered.

"Oh, we'll give you a hundred bucks or so," he offered.

Those words, at that point, were almost enough to kill the whole idea for me. I lacked the experience of how to use such a lofty sum, so I looked at it from a purely business point of view and realized that this "hundred bucks or so" would not get me very far. I was to understand only later that it was not the money, but the commitment that I needed. But that realization did not dawn on me for many years. And so, for the time being, the concept of the Stratford Shakespearean Festival was put on the shelf.

With a Veterans' Affairs grant in my pocket, I enrolled in Trinity College at the University of Toronto for my B.A. I graduated in 1948. During this period, I married my first wife, Robin. We lived on Toronto Island, and it was there that our first son, Robert, was born. One of our neighbours was Cliff Daniels, who was just starting a new magazine for Maclean Hunter called *Civic Adminstration*. He invited me to join him, which I gladly did, even though it meant writing about such dramatic subjects as road-making machinery, sewage disposal plants, and the like. I soon discovered that the people who are involved with sewage disposal plants treat them like jewels. I found myself on cat-walks, dangling over the flushings of thousands of fellow Canadians, interviewing men about how they worked.

It sounds like a dictionary definition of the word "inauspicious," in terms of the creation of a theatre festival, but it was through my journalistic work for that magazine that I found myself, in the spring of 1951, in Winnipeg, covering a conference of the Canadian section of the American Waterworks Association. When I arrived in the prairie city, I soon discovered the latest mayor of Stratford was already there.

Mayor David Simpson was determinedly trying to make

an impression and lead people to believe that Stratford, Ontario, was a good place to visit and live. An earlier mayor had not left a very good reputation, and memories of the strike still loomed over the town. At one point during the convention, Simpson threw a party for a large number of the delegates. As I was both from Stratford and a member of the press, naturally I was invited.

Even though it was a waterworks convention, not much water was consumed at the party. Mayor Simpson waxed enthusiastically and, I must say, rather freely about the advantages of Stratford. So I thought it would be a good time to resurrect the idea of the Festival.

"Mayor, what do you think about a Shakespearean Festival in Stratford?" I asked him.

"It sounds like a great idea to me," Simpson replied. "I don't know anything about Shakespeare, except that it's the name of a school on the east end of town. But if it's good for Stratford, then I'm all for it. See what you can do."

For the first time, I found myself saying aloud, "Jesus, this is *it*!" And, there and then, I decided to concentrate on making the Festival happen. Years before, I had been put off with the offer of a hundred dollars. This time, there was no offer of money, but there was a sense of commitment. It was the real beginning.

I returned to Toronto, and on the strength of the recommendation from the mayor of Stratford, I went to work. I was in the "publishing business," so I had a lot more contacts with government officials and the press than I had had a few years before. I was also a lot older; I was just turning thirty-one.

I promptly approached the Minister of Tourism in Ontario, the Minister of Education, and Celia Franca, who had recently arrived in Canada to found the National Ballet of Canada. I then went back to Mayor Simpson and told him such things as, "Well, you know, I was talking to Dr. W.J. Dunlop (Ontario's education minister), and he thinks a Shakespearean Festival is a great idea."

True, people like Celia Franca had neither money nor time to spare, but I "used" her name, and this was crucial. (I could never get away with something like that today because

Stratfordians have all seen these famous people for over three decades, each summer, and would know that I was exaggerating their support.)

Not unlike the story of the Hollywood producer who tells a famous director that he has a certain star, and then tells the famous star that he has a certain director, and thus manages to put together a deal, I used both sides against the middle. For instance, I met with Dana Porter, the right-hand man of Premier Leslie Frost, (and the father of the now-famous lawyer and Stratford Festival board member Julian Porter) and told him, "The mayor of Stratford has asked me to get working on a Shakespearean Festival. We're setting up a committee, and I hope I have your support."

And then I reported to the Mayor, "The Honourable Dana Porter thinks it's a wonderful concept for the city and the province." In this way, slowly but surely, more and more people became involved. (Dana Porter eventually became a strong backer of the Festival.)

I was fortunate, in retrospect, that the waterworks convention had taken place in May, since it gave me a good excuse not to report back to the Mayor immediately. "It's summer," I told him, "and most people are away from Toronto on vacation." This bought me valuable time to line up many more people over a number of months.

I quickly learned that nobody can say that a Shakespearean Festival is a bad thing; you are a Philistine if you do. I made sure I never asked these eminent people for anything. I just told them what we were planning to do, hoping that they would say, "That's a fantastic idea," or "That's magnificent."

From the second beginning, in 1951, I used my role as a writer for *Civic Administration* magazine in order to get my foot in the door. Once I was in the offices of the various cabinet ministers, I never used subterfuge; I went right ahead and stated my concept of a Shakespearean Festival in Stratford.

It is hard to describe the exact moment that the Festival went from being merely my good idea to being my obsession. Over the post-war years, I had grown in confidence, keeping pace with Canada's growing sense of confidence. I had gone from no training in my civilian life to being a writer for a major publishing firm, Maclean Hunter. This was pretty exciting for a young man from a town of less than twenty thousand people, and I had begun to feel that the world was my oyster; that I could do anything.

Canada had also changed considerably. It did not happen immediately after the war, since everyone was looking after the people who had returned from battle, and the veterans themselves were busy trying to get into some kind of normal harness again. But within a few years, after many had gone to university, a new maturity and feeling of self-worth was sweeping the land.

Quite simply, one thing led to another until I was obsessed. I kept visiting major political leaders and deans of the arts, and reporting back to Dave Simpson in Stratford, "I just talked with such-and-such, and he thinks that a Stratford Festival is a terrific idea."

Mayor Simpson would exclaim, "Jesus, Tom, that's fantastic!"

Soon, he told me, "I think that the Chamber of Commerce would support this."

The statement was silly, in retrospect, but it allowed me to return to the "big names" outside, and declare, "Sir, you asked me to keep you informed on the development of the Stratford Shakespearean Festival, so I thought you would like to know that, as a result of the mayor's urging, the Chamber of Commerce has set up a committee to investigate the idea."

By late 1951, I *knew* that the Festival was going to happen, because I was going to *make* it happen.

3

A Hundred and Twenty-Five Dollars

In retrospect, I can see that it was my experience with the press that led to my personal breakthrough with the Stratford Shakespearean Festival concept. It had been wrong of me to ask the mayor for money back in 1945. I should have merely asked him to support the idea, so that I could tell others that I had the mayor's support. Then that person could not fail to give me his or her support.

That was the clue, and from the moment I realized that, I never asked anybody for anything except their support. Although it sounds almost comical today, in the early 1950s, for some local, small-town Stratfordian to talk to the Minister of Education of the province of Ontario was pretty impressive. I never had to worry about anyone in the town ever checking with the ministry, because they knew damned well that they could not get through. Communications were not then what they are now, and that fact worked strongly in my favour.

I solicited such support for a number of months in late 1951, and the idea grew bigger and bigger. I travelled to Stratford every weekend from my home in Ajax, where we had recently moved, and stayed at my mother's place. I used to sit at the phone every weekend and call up people in Stratford, stating, "It's Tom. I talked to the Minister of Tourism and to Celia Franca of the National Ballet, and I've done this and that and the other thing, and I'd like you to get involved in this Festival."

The support was surprisingly strong, in that no one ever seemed to object to the idea. My mother, however, worried that things were going too easily, and that I was getting too excited. As a third-generation Stratford native, she knew everyone in town, knew all their backgrounds, knew all the dirty laundry in their closets. She was sure that there must be some objection out there, somewhere, and she kept suggesting that I phone people whom she thought would be very hard-headed about it and would bring me back to earth a bit. She did not realize that everyone had to say "yes," because it was Shakespeare, so she kept throwing names at me of people who would be a lot tougher: Stratford financiers, bank managers, the head of the local trust company, and so on. She was sure that they would want to can it right away, but she was wrong. Even the toughest said "yes," whether they meant it or not.

Another reason why everyone was so encouraging about the project was the fact that they did not think it would happen – or, if it did, that it would end up as a small group performing Shakespeare in a barn, somewhere on the outskirts of town. But this was not the main reason for the support I received, not by a long shot. For every man and woman who thought "Sure, encourage the guy; it'll never come to be anyway," there was another who felt it really would come to fruition.

My mother (my father died in 1942, while I was in Europe) and my first wife, Robin, were the first to really understand the scope of what I was trying to do. As the project took on more reality – in my own mind, at least – my mother became ever more encouraging. She would often phone me in Toronto to tell me about someone who was coming to Stratford as a speaker, or someone else I should talk to.

It was as a result of one of her calls that I enlisted the support of the orchestra conductor Boyd Neel. His Boyd Neel Orchestra had achieved great success in England, and he was now touring Canada for the first time. He was here under the auspices of Columbia Artists Management which ran Community Concerts of Canada, an organization that set up community groups to sponsor Columbia's artists. That year my mother was president of the Stratford branch. She made an appointment for me to see Neel at the Queen's Hotel in Stratford where he was staying.

I went with some trepidation. After all, this was my first meeting with an international star, and one from Shakespeare's native land. Would he be condescending about an ex-colony presuming to mount a major Shakespearean Festival in a small town, even though it was called "Stratford"?

We sat in the lobby of the hotel and I outlined the whole idea with great enthusiasm, throwing in the idea that we could also present music during the Festival. To my delight, he was even more interested in my idea than several of the Canadians I had talked with had been. Our conversation gave me a great boost. Now I could say that an international star from England agreed with the idea, and I also had the feeling inside that he really meant his enthusiasm.

It was a very pleasant conclusion to this conversation when Boyd Neel, having moved to Canada in the meantime, conducted his Hart House orchestra at the Stratford Festival just three years later.

It was an exhausting few months. I was spending a lot of time on the office phone at Maclean Hunter and then driving out to Stratford after work each day, which took nearly two hours, to drum up support. Then I would drive back home to Ajax, which lies northeast of Toronto, often arriving at two or three in the morning and then be at work at my magazine job by nine. This pace continued until I finally gave up my job and moved back to Stratford when the Festival began to heat up.

A turning point came when, one Saturday I was in Stratford, I encountered Fred Cox, an alderman, on the street. I had spoken with him previously, of course, as a private citizen, and he was all for a Festival, being a promoter-type, anyway.

"Goddamit, Tom," Fred told me with some force. "You're going to *have* to go to the City Council with this thing. Everywhere they go in town, now, they keep hearing about this idea of a Festival, and you haven't gone to them, yet. They're going to get mad, if you don't."

"Okay," I replied. "When's the next meeting?"

By happy circumstance, there was one planned for that Monday night, just two days later. I phoned Maclean Hunter in Toronto and got the day off. I realized at once that this was the one time that I *had* to ask for something. But there was a catch. If I did not request financial support, it would seem as though the project was not serious, while if I asked for too much money, they would turn it down and effectively kill it.

(I also knew that, if the Festival began to look as if it might happen, the City Council would back off for political reasons. They would be worried that if they showed support they might lose many votes since there would be opposition in town. My reasoning proved correct. The City Council quickly stepped aside and encouraged me to go to the Chamber of Commerce and set up a Stratford Festival Committee.)

Like any good impresario, I went to my mother for advice. "What do I ask for?" I queried, with some concern.

She sat down at the kitchen table, and in her imagination she went around the Council table murmuring, "Well, *that* one will go for it." "*He'll* be tough." "Yes, *he* might agree; he's English." "Yeah, *he'll* be alright." "*This* one I don't know."

And so it went, as she talked through the entire Stratford City Council – she knew them all. Then she came to the same conclusion that I had reached. "Tom, look. If you ask for too little, they'll give it to you just to get rid of you, and it won't seem important. They'll do it to get you out of the way. But you can't ask for too much either. It's clear that you've got to ask for the right amount, and I think that the right amount is a hundred dollars."

It was then that I realized that a straight business approach would not work. Inflation had not yet reached 1970s' proportions, but this hundred dollars would still not get me as much as the original "hundred bucks or so" that had been offered years before. In fact, any amount that it was reasonable to expect from the city would not go very far. It was the *commitment* that was important, and I kept this belief throughout the campaign. I would often be accused of being "unbusiness-like," and rightly so. But a straight business approach would never have resulted in the Festival.

So I attended the meeting of the City Council, in late January 1952. A number of delegations preceded me, such as the Red Cross and the Humane Society, as well as quite a few important Stratfordians all asking for money for their favourite charities.

And there I was, with no committee, no nothing, and by this time I had been out of Stratford for most of the preceding decade because of the war, university, and the stint at Maclean Hunter. The council had changed over that period, and my old friends were no longer there.

The Chairman, Lawrence Feick, who was thin, quiet, and business-like, and who, as I recall, worked in a furniture factory, called me in, saying, "I hope that you're not going to take very long, Tom, because we've got a big agenda." He was not harsh, nor was he hustling me, but when he said that, I knew that he meant every word.

"No, I won't," I replied, appreciating his honesty.

I looked around at the faces of the all-male group, who were sitting about, all of them in suits and ties. There was Bert Davies, an Englishman, always very dapper in his dress, who was involved with the amateur operetta society in Stratford. He worked in the CN shops, as did Art Skidmore and Dan McKenzie, the latter well-known for his athletic abilities. Dutch Meier was also present; he was plump, with a great sense of humour. He distributed vending machines and later became mayor of Stratford. He would always be a strong supporter of the Festival. There was a man named Henry Palmer, too, who was small-built, and had an old-fashioned mustache. I remember him, because he was a Briton, and the one my mother was referring to, when she said, "He'll go for it; he's a limey." And there was Roy Tompkins, tall, thick-set, a Stratford industrialist, whose wife, Fran, later became the secretary to the Stratford Foundation, a position she would hold for over three decades.

I took a deep breath and began my spiel. "Gentlemen, I want to get a Shakespearean Festival going, the best in the world. I think that it will attract people here from all over the globe, and we'll have trains bringing school kids in. I want a hundred dollars to go to New York to get Sir Laurence Olivier."

My presentation took less than five minutes.

Why Olivier? Because he was the greatest Shakespearean actor of that era, and I believed that Olivier could not *not* be interested in a Shakespearean Festival. Also, he happened to be performing on Broadway at that time. (I had done my homework, I must admit.) I knew that he was doing the two Cleopatras, Shakespeare's and Shaw's, in repertoire in New York, and I figured that he was not only the best guy, he was also the closest.

When I was challenged by an alderman, Stan Tapley, the manager of the local radio station in Stratford, CJCS, who pointedly asked, "What's your interest in this thing?" I said, flatly, "I want to be general manager." That stumped the aldermen, as they had not expected me to tell them exactly what I desired. The naked truth usually stuns people, does it not? (Tapley told me after the Stratford Festival opened, "Listening to you that night at that City Council meeting, I thought you were either drunk or crazy.")

Finally, another alderman, Wilf Gregory, spoke up. He was slightly balding, tall, ramrod straight, and very distinguished. He was with British Mortgage, a trust company, and would be the only one of all these men who would serve on the Stratford Festival board. Indeed, Gregory eventually became its president.

"You know," said Wilf, "a hundred dollars to go to New York doesn't sound like very much to me. I vote that we make it hundred and twenty-five." The vote passed, and I got the money.

Now I *had* to go ahead with the Festival; my bluff had been called. Back at my mother's home later that night, I found her frightened, but as supportive as any woman who had once let her teenage son be locked up in a jail cell every night for a week to research the lives of hobos.

"Well, hell; you can only *try*," she told me, looking very scared.

But was I scared? Not on your life! I was elated. I knew from that moment on, the Stratford Festival would happen. I never doubted it for an instant.

§

Fortunately, there were more people than just myself who would "only try." The support of the local and, literally overnight, the national press was unwavering and almost overwhelming.

"PLAN WINS FAVOR" read the headline in the Stratford *Beacon-Herald*, on January 22, 1952. "COUNCIL TOLD OF IDEA TO MAKE STRATFORD WORLD FAMOUS SHAKESPEAREAN CENTRE" read the smaller heading. Some of the paragraphs from that article are worth quoting: "Dreams of Stratford as an even greater cultural centre [!] were unfolded at a regular meeting of City Council on Monday night and the possibilities were presented in so enthusiastic a manner that up to $125 traveling expenses were approved for further investigation.

"Thomas Patterson, associate editor of a Toronto publication [thank you] and a former Stratford resident [no thanks], appeared before Council and outlined a cultural program for Stratford that would make the city world famous as a Shakespearean centre and mean thousands of extra dollars for the city, he felt."

Other discussions at that meeting, according to the local paper, included the pleasantly absurd (the Shakespearean Festival "would involve an estimated cost of $100,000") and the remarkably prescient ("Mr. Patterson felt that perhaps a Shakespearean company could be formed and go on tour" – a thought fulfilled by the creation of the Canadian Players in 1954).

The conclusion of the lengthy, first-page article is charming in both its honesty and its small-town sense of financing: "From an industrial standpoint Stratford has been at a standstill," said Alderman Bert Davies, "and if we can build it up as a cultural centre, I certainly think we are on the right track. I'm in favour of an investigation into its possibilities and having Mr. Patterson bring his report back to Council." The final paragraph reads, "The other members of the Council all agreed that it was worth investigating, and not one voice was raised against the up-to-$125 expense money."

Now, if this was all the publicity that this little Stratford Council meeting received, it would have been minor, indeed.

But the Canadian Press wire picked it up, and it suddenly appeared in papers across Canada:

"CANADIAN DRAMA CENTRE" read the headline in the Timmins *Press*. "AMERICAN CENTRE OF DRAMA," declared *The St. Catharines Standard*. "PLAN DRAMA CENTRE AT STRATFORD, ONT.," proclaimed the Port Arthur *News Chronicle*.

It must be admitted that I had used my time well at *Civic Administration*. While on trips covering such things as the Ontario Safety Conference or the Good Roads Convention in such places as Chatham or Sudbury, I would always make a point of getting the local reporter aside at lunch breaks and, with the help of a drink, would let them in on the story. (Newspaper reporters were not paid well in those days and were delighted to be entertained by a "big city" reporter.) So when the news of the Festival began to flow out of Stratford, many of them already had the background to write their own stories and not just take it off the Canadian Press wire. It was not only news articles which appeared; there were also friendly editorials, many of them also picked up and run in other major papers across Canada.

The local *Beacon-Herald* was the most sober, yet still sympathetic: "In planning the project, the practical side may well prove more difficult than the winning of approval for what is undoubtedly a challenge of unusual dimensions for a community of Stratford's resources," it stated in an editorial titled "NEEDS FUNDS AS WELL AS FAITH." "The final decision to attempt so ambitious a task should, we submit, be made only in the light of full knowledge of its varied details – and with entire recognition of the difficulties to be expected. We should like to see assured funds commensurate with Mr. Patterson's faith before advising the plunge."

An editorial in the London *Free Press* the following day was typically generous: "More power to the City Council of Stratford, where the lovely river park, the bells and the swans have long been an example to less aesthetic municipalities. Now perhaps a like impetus will come to the theatre, from the same quarter."

Even such a politically important newspaper as the Ottawa *Journal* printed an editorial which effused, "What could be more logical than that Stratford-on-Avon [sic], with its picturesque setting on the banks of the lake which divides the city almost in two equal parts, should aspire to be the Shakespearean Centre of Canada. The setting is perfect." (The fact that the *Journal* was merely reprinting an editorial that had previously appeared in the Woodstock *Daily Sentinel-Review*, and originally in the Moose Jaw *Times-Herald*, whose editor was a former Stratfordian, is not the point – the bigwigs in the nation's capital were reading about the concept.)

There was a further advantage to all this extraordinary publicity from one Stratford City Council meeting. Maclean Hunter ran the Canadian Press clipping services, and my magazine, *Civic Administration*, received all of the clippings that mentioned my name. So I kept receiving, at no cost, all the articles and editorials on the Festival. I decided to make a press book out of it all, which I could carry with me. Moose Jaw was one thing; but with a lengthy editorial in the St. John's, Newfoundland, paper as well, how could I fail to impress the Powers That Were in New York City? (Or so the small-town Canadian boy thought.)

I know it may sound like bragging, and it is perhaps a sign of my naïvety, but all this publicity never fazed me. I had absolutely no self-doubts whatsoever. I have never been afraid of being embarrassed in front of important people. (I was not shaken by sharing that car with Sir Anthony Eden.) Indeed, I would have been more worried if there had been no publicity!

In the last week of January 1952, I found myself in possession of a fat scrapbook and the impressive sum of $125 to spend. I must have spent over half of it on long-distance calls to New York, trying to reach Sir Laurence Olivier. But I never talked to him. I finally reached his secretary at the Algonquin Hotel, where his office was located. I had long and fine conversations with her, and she was very pleasant, but there was simply no way that I was going to see Olivier.

I finally came to the conclusion that the only way to accomplish my goal was to go down to New York, tell the secretary that I was down there for some other reason, and insist that Olivier just had to see me. It just shows the vanity and the egotism I had at that time. Not to mention optimism.

So I went to New York and stayed at the Algonquin Hotel, hoping that I would be fortunate enough to meet Sir Laurence in the elevator. (I had been to New York once previously, and it was hardly an auspicious visit. A year after the war ended, I had gone back to Europe on a flight that had developed a problem and had been forced to land in New York. In those days there was a currency restriction, and I had a few pounds on me, some Canadian dollars, but only ten cents in American money. Since I had no visa and little money, one of New York's finest was called. He arrived carrying a machine gun, took my luggage, and escorted me across the airport in a police car to the Air Canada plane. That was the sum total of my experience of New York City.)

I discovered that Olivier had left the Algonquin some two weeks earlier to move to an apartment. So I phoned up his secretary and announced, more or less, "Here I am! Won't Sir Laurence be happy to see me?"

He was not.

It turned out that the great actor had a very good reason why he had no time to see this Canadian. He was not only acting in the two Cleopatras in repertory, but he was commuting each day to Philadelphia, where he was directing another play. He had few minutes to spare for anyone, much less me.

I was pretty desperate, sitting in my expensive bedroom in the Algonquin. So I got the New York telephone directory, and, starting with the As, I began going through it to see if I could find a famous name I could call. Then I saw something else.

On the telephone stand was a book of matches advertising the Algonquin Hotel, and at the bottom of it was the name "Ben B. Bodney, President." So I figured, Ben's my man! I knew that the Algonquin was frequented by such "regulars" as George S. Kaufman, Dorothy Parker, and S.J. Perelman, and that actors used to stay across the street at the far cheaper Royalton Hotel and arrange to meet people at the Algonquin in order to impress them. So I phoned Bodney up, and said that I would like to see him about this project, and I thought he could help me with it. I had been trying to get Olivier, I explained, but he was too busy.

"I'm just going to bed now," Bodney told me.

I looked at my watch; it was five in the afternoon.

"My busy time is at midnight," he explained. "I'll see you at twelve tonight."

I said, "Fine," told him that I was bald, and described the clothes I was wearing. "I'll be at the bottom of the elevator at midnight," I promised.

When the chosen time arrived, Mr. Bodney came off the elevator, and I launched into a description of my project for Stratford, Ontario. "Mr. Bodney," I pleaded. "I have to go back to my City Council with *something! Anything!"*

He thought for a few seconds and then said, "Well, there's an agent coming in here in about five or ten minutes. Why don't you go over and have a drink, and I'll send him to you?"

While I was nursing my drink, a sleazy agent came in. He was the epitome of the Hollywood image of a Broadway agent: waxed moustache, waxed hair, dapper clothes. He joined me, and I outlined the project to him and told him how I had tried to get hold of Olivier but had failed to do so.

"Who do you want?" he asked me. "Cedric Hardwick? Charles Laughton? Why not take a Broadway company? They're not doing anything in the summertime, anyway."

"Yeah, that sounds great," I said. I certainly did not want to deal with this fellow, but he was offering me that "something" to take back to Stratford, even though it was not what I wanted.

Then he asked me, "Say, how's the oil doing up there in Canada?" The rest of our discussion was about the tar sands in Alberta.

The following morning, I tried my one, last wild card. True, I "had" Hardwick, Laughton, and a whole Broadway company – "my choice," in the words of the Broadway agent. But I turned to, at last, my "research" from home. Shortly before I had left for New York, I had gone to the Stratford Public Library and read the annual reports of various foundations in the United States: the Carnegie, the Rockefeller, and so on. I went through the list of officers of each, and picked out those who looked like they might be in a position to help me. I gathered my clippings from the newspapers of Canada, and went off to the Carnegie Foundation. I had no introduction and no appointment.

I approached the secretary and asked to see the head of the British Empire and Commonwealth Division.

"Your name?"

"Tom Patterson," I declared firmly, as if they should know who I was.

"One moment please."

"That's Tom Patterson from Stratford, Canada!" I added.

Five minutes later, a young woman came out and said, "He will see you now."

I went into the office of this man and explained the project. To show the support that it had in Canada, I showed him all the clippings in my press book. The book was so amateurishly done (it is in the Stratford Festival Archives to this day) that it looked like a schoolkid's album.

My feelings were, then, as always, "How am I going to sell my idea to this guy?" My belief in the idea of the Festival conquered any intimidation I probably should have felt. In short, my attitude was "If this fellow won't go along with me, he'll be sorry."

The man read my press book and smiled.

"I think you can appreciate, Mr. Patterson, that we can't get into the business of supporting one town against another. And this is obviously a promotion for Stratford, Ontario."

It was clear that I would not get any money out of him, but I thought that I may as well talk with him anyway. An hour later, after we had spoken in depth on how foundations worked, I left. I was aware that I did not have a briefcase, merely this corny scrap-book tied together with string. I found a place on Sixth Avenue where I bought a briefcase for six dollars, so I would look impressive. It was made of real leather, and it is still my proud possession.

I next went to the Rockefeller Foundation, practising my speech as I went along: The City Council of Stratford is supporting me. We want to do this. It is the right time. Canada is wealthy. (Although I never mentioned money, to be sure.)

With all the troops back from overseas, this is the time to do it. (On this last point, I was absolutely correct, as it turned out.)

"I would like to see Mr. Charles Fahs," I told the secretary.

"Your name, please?"

"Tom Patterson. From Stratford, Canada."

Thank God for the annual report of the Rockefeller Foundation in the Stratford Library. Within five minutes, I was sitting and talking with Charles Fahs in his office. This time, I kept my scrapbook in my briefcase as I once again outlined the idea of a Shakespearean Festival. I believe that I added quite a bit of enthusiasm to this retelling, because when I finished, Charles Fahs gave me my most promising response yet.

"Yes, this is the kind of thing that we could be interested in," he said with a twinkle in his eye. "Please let me know how you get along."

I know that it does not sound like much, but that brief sentence, "Please let me know how you get along" was really all I wanted. They were key words, and they allowed me to return to Stratford and report to City Council. I had an immense sense of relief that I had accomplished something, although I was well aware that it just stopped a gap at this point. I knew that I was not interested in Hardwick, Laughton, or any Broadway company. They were big names, it was true, but only as actors, and I was looking for a big-name Artistic Director. Anyway, I did not want to be beholden to the New York agent.

When I got back home, I told the council members, "I'm very sorry. Sir Laurence Olivier can't come because he is too tied up and is committed for the next two years, and we want someone before that. But we could have Charles Laughton, Cedric Hardwick, even a Broadway company. And the Rockefeller Foundation is interested."

"ROCKEFELLER FOUNDATION TO CONSIDER FESTIVAL PROPOSAL," read the headline in the next edition of the Stratford *Beacon-Herald*. The article was truthful, but only when it quoted me directly. "Mr. Patterson made the trip, and while he was unable to obtain the services of Sir Laurence, he did receive his blessing, he said. 'Sir Laurence,' he said, 'is unable to take an active interest because of other obligations. We were reaching for the moon in trying to get Sir Laurence, but we will settle for a star,' [Patterson] added."

When I got home that night, my wife asked me, "What are you going to do now?"

"Nobody in New York reads the Stratford *Beacon-Herald*," I told her.*

---

*It was not until two years later, during the second year of the Festival, that the Rockefeller Foundation gave money to us. They sent representatives up for opening night, and after the performance and party, I invited them back to my house. John Marshall, now in charge of their "Stratford project," came with a wonderful woman named Flora Rhind. I asked her how she enjoyed the show and whether she was happy with their grant. I then related the story of my first visit to the Rockefeller Foundation in New York and ended with the punchline, "Nobody in New York reads *The Beacon-Herald*."

"Oh yes they do," Flora Rhind said. "I saw that clipping, and I shoved it in my desk. I didn't let Mr. Fahs see it, because I knew exactly what you were doing!"

4

The Getting of Guthrie

The Stratford City Council was satisfied that their $125 investment had been well spent. I received assurance from the councillors that "everything possible would be done to assist [me]" in my plans. A representative from the Stratford Chamber of Commerce also appeared at the meeting and presented a report from the committee that had been set up to look into the Shakespearean Festival project. The committee recommended that authority be given to set up a committee of citizens at large to handle the project, independent of the City Council. It was this body that eventually evolved into the Stratford Shakespearean Festival Foundation of Canada.

The Globe and Mail of Toronto, then as now the most widely read paper in the country, reported the meeting. "Thomas Patterson, one of those interested, told a city council committee that Olivier had said the plan should 'go over.' He said that in New York he had been told by theatrical spokesmen that talent for any drama would be available." Fortunately, *The Globe and Mail* never made a retraction regarding my untruths. But if that sleazy Broadway agent had seen the paper, he would have been very flattered to be labelled a legitimate "theatrical spokesman"!

I was very uncomfortable about lying, but I was working from a simple, if slightly unethical principle: One did not have to talk to Sir Laurence Olivier to know that he would be all for a Shakespearean Festival! Indeed, I probably even talked myself into believing that it was the truth, and that I had, indeed, met with him on my New York trip.

One happy consequence of the initial publicity the festival project received resulted from a brief CBC News Roundup, which had been broadcast following Earl Cameron's reading of "The National" one night. It attracted someone who would turn out to be extremely valuable – an American listener to our Canadian airwaves.

Today's news carries the story of a plan to develop a Shakespearean Centre in this western Ontario city of Stratford. The choice of a site is a happy one.

This Stratford in Perth County, like the Stratford in Warwickshire, England, is situated on the Avon River. To be sure, we pronounce the name Avon, while in England it is A-von.

This Stratford in Ontario, with a population of 18,878 at last count, treasures its connection with the older Stratford. The founders laid it out as a living memorial to Shakespeare. Many of its wards and public schools carry names familiar in his plays. Children in Stratford learn the three Rs at Hamlet, Falstaff, Romeo, and Juliet School – or else at Shakespeare, Anne Hathaway, or Avon School.

A Stratford feature, as well known as its furniture industry and its CNR shops, is the park system which extends for a mile along the Avon, just one block from the main business section.

At the heart of the city, back of the post office, is a shell bandstand in a natural amphitheatre, suitable for outdoor programs. From here the park extends in both directions. One beauty spot is the Shakespearean Garden, built on the site of a burned mill. A sundial, unveiled by Lord Tweedsmuir, counts the hours here. Presiding over the garden is a bust of Shakespeare by the modern sculptor Cleeve Horn, presented by the Sons of England across Canada.

Over the road and down a flight of stone steps is another sundial, a gift of the Rotary Club of Stratford-upon-Avon, England, to its namesake here. It is in sight of a swimming pool provided by the Lions Club.

At the other end of the park mile is Queen's Park, a spacious area of trees and grass and picnic tables, with a sports field nearby, and for good measure, a Normal School whose tradition for many years included presentation of a Shakespearean play annually.

This, in brief, is the background of the Classic City in which this Shakespearean Centre project is the big question today.

It may sound like very much to do about nothing, in retrospect, but it was hardly that in the heady, winter days of 1952. A professor of speech and drama at the Edinboro State Teachers' College in Pennsylvania, Lawrence Vincent, heard that CBC radio broadcast. He was as excited as could be about the idea of a Shakespearean Festival and phoned me at my home in Ajax, Ontario.

"Could I come up in the Easter break? I would like to talk to you about it," he requested. When he finally did arrive, in early April, he turned out to be one of my best propagandists. Why? Because I had told the City Council that people would come from all over the world to this potential Festival; they had given me a generous $125 to spend; and here was an honest-to-goodness drama professor from an American university (no matter how small or insignificant). By the time Vincent arrived in Stratford, he had been elevated by my publicity to a professor of theatre at a major American university. And who was going to challenge that? I could not admit that he taught at a mere teachers' college; there was one in Stratford, for heaven's sake!

When Vincent flew in, I took him to visit Stratford. It was soon clear that he had thought the project was far more advanced than it was. And he was very frank in stating that he wanted a job in this exciting project. I am in no way being critical of him in writing that; for even when he realized that it was far too soon to expect anything of the kind, he was still anxious to help in any way that he could.

Which he did, in ways he never imagined. I told him that he could give interviews in Stratford, and he gave a number – marvellously. Indeed, Vincent was the first one who nixed my original idea of holding the plays in open air in the town's band shell, which had a natural amphitheatre. "No, you can't do it in the open air," he warned me – as Tony Guthrie would again warn me, some months later. "You know, the birds!"

The Beacon-Herald treated him as if he were a world-class theatre scholar. "SAYS STRATFORD COULD BECOME GREAT SHAKESPEAREAN CENTRE" cried the headline in the local paper, on April 7, 1952. "If Stratford people are sufficiently 'dedicated' to the idea of building a Shakespearean Festival here, nothing can prevent this city from becoming the Shakespearean centre for all Canada, in the opinion of Lawrence Vincent, who came to the city over the weekend from Edinboro, Pa., to discuss the project with Tom Patterson."

The article went on to quote the Yankee enthusiast at length, and he never seemed to say anything but the right thing. "If that larger aim [of seeing the Festival as something for all of Canada, and not merely for one city] is desired by the people of Stratford, they will not be left alone in this great effort. There are people and organizations all over the continent to help. They are not going to help, though, if the idea is just to make money."

Vincent also noted that those who thought that they could not afford a theatre were under the false assumption that it was a "luxury." Like great music, great drama had been found to be a necessity. Yanking Stratfordians by their Anglophile heartstrings, Vincent noted that Great Britain, "in its hour of greatest trial, had founded its Arts Council. It was because the English people realized that they were not people of that little island alone, but a part of eternity." (You will be pleased to know that Vincent came back to Stratford several years later to visit the by-then successful Festival.)

Lawrence Vincent, like many Americans who pick up our excellent public radio system, had become obsessed with the "Stage" series. He listened to CBC from morning until night, and he even expressed interest in emigrating to Canada. I offered to take him to see Mavor Moore, whom I did not know personally, although I was well aware that he was important. Moore and others were in downtown Toronto at that time, setting up what would become Canadian television.

I phoned up the prominent actor/director/playwright (and future Stratford Shakespearean Festival performer) and said, "I've got this guy here. Could I bring him to see you? He would like to come up to Canada to act, and he's a great admirer of yours." It was the farthest thing from my mind that this meeting with Mavor would prove to be the vital link in an extraordinary series of connections – connections that resulted in Tyrone Guthrie's and Alec Guinness's participation in the Festival.

When I met Mavor Moore for the first time, I outlined the idea for the Festival because he had not heard of it. "Have you talked to my mother?" he asked. I admitted that I had not. "You should certainly talk to her," he told me, and I agreed.

Dora Mavor Moore, one of Canada's premier actresses and directors, and the founder of the seminal New Play Society of Toronto, was in the Society's office on Yonge Street. Mavor phoned her and arranged for us to meet. Her office was small and cluttered. It was on the second story of a building, right beside the Uptown movie theatre, then, as now, one of the major film houses in Canada. For some strange reason, she was wearing a ratty-looking fur, which was still a prominent part of her wardrobe many years later. There were papers and letters piled everywhere, and there was an acting class going on, just a few feet away.

Dora had a funny, cackling giggle, which I found charming, and she took me seriously, which was even more charming. We had a real rapport from the start, even though our first, crucial meeting took less than ten minutes. Surprisingly, she, like her son Mavor, had neither seen nor heard of the prospective Stratford Festival. I described my project, and told her how I was unable to get Olivier. In reply, she gave me what was the single most important suggestion of my years of struggle to create a Festival in Stratford.

"As far as I'm concerned, the greatest Shakespearean director in the world is Tyrone Guthrie," she said.

"Good! Let's get him!" I enthused, not knowing who on earth the man was, but sounding as sure as a child lining up a chum across the street to play with.

"Fine," Mrs. Moore said. "I'll write a letter to John Coulter" (the fine Canadian playwright who was in England at that time, trying to get Guthrie to direct his greatest play, *Riel*). I thanked her, took Lawrence Vincent back to where he was staying, and rushed over to the nearest Toronto library to look in *Who's Who in British Theatre* to find out who this fellow Guthrie was.

It is really quite amazing that I had not heard of the man. It was if someone wishing to begin a film festival in 1952 had never heard of Orson Welles. Famed as the man in charge of productions at London's celebrated Old Vic Theatre between 1933 and 1945, and as administrator of the Old Vic Sadler's Wells organization from 1939 to 1945 and again in 1951 and 1952, Tyrone Guthrie had staged a number of major plays on London's West End, on Broadway, and, yes, he had even directed my "close, personal friend" Charles Laughton in a number of Shakespearean plays in the early 1930s. He had also, not coincidentally, directed some plays by the Scottish dramatist, James Bridie, Dora Mavor Moore's uncle.

True to her word, Mrs. Moore wrote to John Coulter, who mentioned the concept to Tyrone Guthrie. The Irish/Scottish director told the Canadian playwright that he would like to hear more about it, and Coulter wrote the same back to Dora Mavor Moore.

By this time, Mrs. Moore and I had grown quite friendly. Over the difficult months to follow, I frequently visited her to keep her informed of our progress, and one day Dora and I phoned Guthrie from her office. We tried to get him at the Old Vic, and were told that he was not there – we should try Edinburgh. But he was not there, either. Edinburgh told us that he had left some days before, and that we should try his home in the village of Annagh-ma Kerrig in Ireland.

When we first got through, the lines were crackling with static. In those days, telephoning was not like it is now with satellites – we could hear all the waves of the ocean. Then, when we finally got through and heard something on the other end of the line, it went dead.

We phoned again, and the line went dead again. On our third try, we finally got through. Guthrie explained later what had happened, in his autobiography, *A Life in the Theatre*.

In the summer of 1952 I was at home in Ireland. One evening the telephone rang and our postmistress told me that earlier that day a call had come for me which purported to be from Toronto.

Mrs. McCabe's answer had been categorical. "Nonsense," she said, hung up and went to feed her hens.

Now, she said, the same joker was on the line again. Would I speak?

"This is Tom Patterson," said a still, small voice out of the everywhere. "Will you come to Canada and give advice? We want to start a Shakespearean festival in Stratford, Ontario. We will pay your expenses and a small fee."

"When do you want me?"

"At once. Tomorrow, if you can."

Naturally, I said yes. I had some time at my disposal. It would be fun to have another look at Canada after all these years. [Many years before, he had been involved in a CBC radio series.] I did not take the advice part or the Shakespearean festival very seriously.

I got out a map. Stratford was about a hundred miles west-southwest of Toronto, rather near to Lake Huron. It was a railway junction. It did not look at all important.

My own recollections are that his question, "When do you want me?" completely threw me, because we had no money. I had outlined the idea, and used my standard sales pitch, with phrases like "Canada has been known for the export of wheat and iron ore, but now that the war is over. . . ."

So all I could sputter in response to his question was "As soon as you can." Guthrie told me to "write me a letter, and I'll write you one, and we'll see what we can arrange."

At the time my wife and I had a tenant who was a secretary. She wanted to type this crucial letter for me because I had done it in rough, with parts scratched out, others put in. She was all ready to type a good copy for me, when, at the last moment, I told her, "No. It's going as is." By this time, I had read that Guthrie was the kind of man who hated communications from lawyers and agents; he wanted them straight from the horse's mouth. So I sent this letter over as it was, with all its corrections, bad mistakes and typing errors.

The letter is in the Stratford Archives. I think it is important enough to quote here, in full, and with mistakes intact – just as Tyrone Guthrie received it, in the spring of 1952.

Dear Mr. Guthrie:

First of all, may I thank you sincerely for the interest you have shown in our proposed Festival. It is most gratifying, especially to me since I feel it justifies my own faith in the idea.

Before talking about the festival specifically, I shall try and give you some background on theatre in this country. These are only my own personal opinions, and since, I must admit, my knowledge of theatre is very slight, can be taken for what they are worth.

As you know, Canada is not yet 100 years old, and being a young country, has spent most of its time looking for bread and butter. As a result, there was no time for any of the arts – and we are therefore very backward in that respect.

I am now jumping about one generation. We have emerged as a leader amongst the "small powers"; become one of the wealthiest nations in the world and are in the midst of a boom such as has never been known in the world before. On top of that, we have a fairly large group who have seen some of the things we are missing. I mean those who have come back from the late war.

As a result of our boom, bread and butter comes fairly easily (although expensive) and we, as a nation, are casting around to find what it is we are missing.

I think we have found it. When a ballet comes to Toronto, it is impossible to obtain seats after about two days of ticket sales; the Metropolitan Opera played to the largest crowd in its history last month (an average of 11,500 per night); Mrs. Mavor Moore's production of Spring Thaw played to nearly 100,000 people in a five week run just concluded. This may not seem exceptional to you, but when you consider that less than five years ago, nothing like this could have been possible, it shows the rapid maturity that is coming to our people.

Even in the Festival idea, this is evident. I have had the idea since I was a young lad in Stratford when I used to listen to band concerts (by the local railway employees band) on the banks of the Avon. After returning from Europe in 1945, I suggested the idea to several people, both in Stratford and outside the city. It was laughed down as being a crack-pot scheme. "You can't do a thing like that in Canada" it was said.

Last year I again suggested it to the Mayor, and he told me to go ahead and get more information. From there, it just 'growed and growed.'

The reason I am going into such detail as this is because of the fact that even many of the older theatrical people in Canada have a very defeatist attitude toward theatre, and are very much on the defensive. I am pleased to say that Mrs. Moore is not one of these people. As you know, she started the New Play Society about five years ago when things looked very black for its success. She has been most enthusiastic about this Festival idea since she first heard of it some months ago. I would also like to say that she has been of inestimable help to me.

Now to get to Stratford. We have a very beautiful parks system which cuts the town in almost two equal halves. It is along the banks of the Avon and any part of it is within at least a half hours walk from the centre of town-parts of it within three minutes.

In one particular section, there is a natural amphitheatre capable of seating up to about 15,000 people, if need be. It is completely surrounded by trees, except on the river side. There would be no distraction from the outside.

The proposal is to hold the Festival in this area (if you agree). The only other thing which has definitely been pledged as far as the artistic side is concerned, is that the city as a whole would 'take part in' the Festival. By that I mean that the local Anglican Deacon has promised that his services (and he feels confident other churches would do the same) would be conducted in Elizabethan form – using the music of that period and the church costume.

As far as the actual production is concerned, I think I probably know as much of the theatre as any one else – which is nothing – and we therefore are more than willing to give you a completely free hand – that is, within a fairly generous budget. You mentioned in your letter to Mrs. Moore that you would 'be interested, if it offers a fresh advance in the production of Shakespeare.'

This is the feeling of the committee to the last man. There is absolutely nothing to start with, so that whoever does produce the Festival will have no traditions to overcome – and what is more, no local thespians who have their own ideas! We do sincerely want to offer you the chance at a 'fresh advance.'

On the organizational side, there is a committee of leading citizens who have shown enthusiastic interest, and a fairly keen sense in getting the thing started. They are the ones, incidentally, who are inviting you to the city.

As well as the committee, the citizens of the city are most enthusiastic. In my original groundwork, I talked to everybody from clerks taking inventory in the basements of stores, painters (who were painting my Mother's house) up to the doctors, lawyers, etc. etc. Everywhere, I got the same reaction – enthusiasm.

Outside of Stratford, the reception was the same. From government officials to financiers, editors (the idea itself, without any promotion, received coverage in papers from Moose Jaw in the west to Saint John, New Brunswick in the east) down to the man on the street. I must admit that many of them were very doubtful as to whether it would ever come off or not, but they still thought it was a wonderful idea.

Now, what is to be done? The primary reason the committee decided to invite you to Stratford was to give them some idea of what the possibilities are. Where the stage should go; how it should be built; what about lighting; what plays and how many (we propose running for about a month if you think this advisable); and other technicalities which you suggest.

As far as the company itself is concerned, we would also like your advice on it. We have been promised substantial support from the J. Arthur Rank organization, and Leonard Brockington, their Canadian president, has suggested that the leading stars could be obtained from England through them. This information is confidential as it has not been confirmed yet. However, Sir Michael Balcon has said that they want "to give every assistance." He has also suggested that you might pay a visit to him after your return from Canada. The Executive vice-president of the company for which I work, Floyd Chalmers, is acting as an 'agent' for us during a visit to England. He is in London now, and if you wanted, you could get in touch with him at Wellington House, 125, Strand, London. This is the location of our London offices.

We would like, as far as possible, to make use of Canadian talent. Mrs. Moore has told me that there is sufficient here along with Canadians who have left this country for lack of opportunity here. Such people as John Collicott, Michael Ney (with the Stratford Company) Ka Hawtrey, and others.

We realize that this may not be possible to start with, although we would like it kept in mind when a company is being chosen.

The other thing we would like is to get something on which to base our budget. I do not mean by this that we expect you to draw up a budget, but by giving us what you would like for the stage, we could take it to a local contractor and find out what the cost would be. Similarly, with lighting, etc.

As for the company itself, we would appreciate your suggestions on some kind of budget.

And even more, we would like you to become interested enough in the project to come out here in 1953 and produce the Festival.

With your permission, I would also like to arrange a press reception for you. This would in all probability take place in Toronto (about 100 miles from Stratford). Also, I would like you to meet some of the people outside of Stratford whose support would be required – men such as Leonard Brockington, Minister of Education Dr.Dunlop, etc.

I hope you will forgive my long ramblings in this letter, but I thought it better to give you as much background as possible as well as what facts there are.

Incidentally, if you like swimming, you might bring your bathing suit. Port Carling, (where Peter Potter is playing) is in the midst of a beautiful lake land.

Looking forward to seeing you in a couple of weeks,

(signed)
Tom Patterson

At the time I wrote that letter to Tyrone Guthrie, I knew precious little about Canadian Theatre. I was unaware of Les Compagnons in Quebec; I had never even seen a production by Dora Mavor Moore's exciting company, the New Play Society, which had performed plays by Morley Callaghan, had created the long-lasting comedy revue *Spring Thaw*, and had done so much more. I had never even seen a Robert Gill production of Shakespeare (or anyone else, for that matter!) at the Hart House Theatre in the University of Toronto. I had heard of Gelinas's hit play, *Tit-Coq*, a Quebecois play which made it to Toronto and Broadway, because it had been widely publicized, but I had not even taken the trouble of seeing it in either language.

I knew of the Dominion Drama Festival and its annual adjudications, but only because the finals were occasionally held in nearby London, Ontario. And I knew of – but had never seen – the London Little Theatre.

But theatre was burgeoning all around us. The National Ballet of Canada was starting up; the Jupiter Theatre in Toronto was about to flower; the Royal Commission on National Development in the Arts, Letters and Sciences, a.k.a. the Massey Report, had come out in 1951 with a recommendation on the formation of a Canada Council, which was eventually set up in 1957.

Still, my instincts seemed to be good ones for someone so ignorant of theatre. I agreed immediately with Dora Mavor

Moore that we needed a British director for my proposed Shakespearean Festival, just as someone setting up a theatre of Russian plays would think of the Moscow Arts Theatre, and someone about to create a festival of Arthur Miller's plays would not move before calling Elia Kazan. It just seemed like the logical thing to do. When starting a world-class festival of Shakespeare plays, you look to the country that gave birth to the playwright.

Interestingly, since the occasional later critic has taken exception to the Stratford Festival's effect on the development of indigenous Canadian theatre, Dora firmly believed that a Festival in Stratford would encourage professionalism in this country. Alas, what she also wanted was the Toronto headquarters of the Festival to be in her offices at the New Play Society.

With this, I never agreed. There would be great fears, throughout 1952 and beyond, that Toronto would use the Festival for its own, nefarious reasons – a feeling that "Toronto would try to take control of everything." (My living in that city for many years did not help, either.) *We All Hate Toronto* was the name of a witty play by Lister Sinclair from this period, and how right he was! I still recall when Stratford's hockey team played in the Junior A OHA hockey finals held in Toronto, before the war. A Toronto referee, who happened to work at the Canada Packer's plant, made what was generally considered to be a "bad call." The headline in *The Beacon-Herald* the following day told it all: "STOCKYARDS STUMBLEBUM" was the description of the hapless referee, and we meant it, too.

It would have been death for the Stratford Festival to have its headquarters in Toronto, even though Dora was most generous in offering her offices for the task. Furthermore, Tyrone Guthrie wanted a completely free hand in casting, and because he did not know Canadian actors, he feared dependence on Dora's input. (Later he did turn down an actor whom Dora Mavor Moore had recommended, which upset her a great deal.)

On June 12, 1952, just thirteen months before the Stratford Shakespearean Festival of Canada would open, I received my first, personal letter from Tyrone Guthrie in reply to my rather endless one, quoted above. He had previously written to Dora Mavor Moore on May 11, before our first telephone conversation. Although it did not seem so seminal at the time, he had expressed to Mrs. Moore some extremely important thoughts: He was "very interested" in her "unofficial" proposal, which had been passed to him from the playwright John Coulter. He was "not very attracted" to what he called "the usual idea of 'pastoral' Shakespeare," meaning "a rather impromptu stage in questionably suitable 'natural surroundings.'" Guthrie was, however, "intensely interested to produce Shakespeare on a stage which might reproduce the actor-audience relations for which he wrote"; that is, when "the audience [is] closely racked *round* the actors."

In Guthrie's reply to my letter, he offered to come after July 4. I just assumed that this offer meant that he was going to take the job. Even if he should later say "no," I felt I would have no trouble whatsoever in talking him into it. I was that confident. Stupid, yes; but confident. So, at the time, for me the most important part of his letter was his passing reference to money: "May I hear your suggestion in respect of my fee?"

I had no idea what to pay him! Here was a man who I had been told was the greatest Shakespearean director in the world. All I was sure of was, I did *not* want to put anything in writing. I feared that Guthrie might take any letter of mine to his agent, so I thought to myself, "I'll call him. That way he'll have to make a decision over the phone. That way, he can't take it and think about it."

So I phoned Tyrone Guthrie on the pretext of another matter – his travel arrangements or something – and mentioned, as much in passing as his request to me: "Oh, incidentally, that question of your fee. . . .Of course we'll look after you while you're here, and pay you five hundred dollars."

There was a long pause, while the ocean crackled and all sorts of other noises came over the phone. Finally, his thin voice came through saying, "Yes, I guess that will be all right." I thought to myself, he is not very happy, but he is going to come to Canada, and we can settle it when he gets out here.

Guthrie came over in early July 1951. But here is the proper place to mention what happened one Sunday morning, after he had spent a full week in Stratford and around the country, visiting theatres.

"Tom," he said. "There's one thing that I'm very embarrassed to ask about. . . .Remember that telephone conversation we had, about my fee?"

"Yes," I said, my knees shaking.

"You know, the line broke down when you mentioned the amount. How much am I getting?"

"Oh, God, Tony!" I exclaimed. "You *didn't* come all the way over here not *knowing* that!"

"Well, I heard the word 'expenses,' so I thought for sure that I could get back home."

"Uh, you know the fee was – and I hate to mention this – but, like, five hundred dollars."

"Yes?" said the first director of the Stratford Festival. "That's fine."

5

"Madly Keen and Very Sensible"

The news of Tyrone Guthrie's planned visit to Stratford was quickly reported in nearly every paper in Canada. "Stratford, Ontario, is going ahead with plans for a two-week festival of Shakespearean drama in August, 1953," wrote Lauretta Thistle in her Music and Drama column in the Ottawa *Citizen* on June 7, 1952.

"TYRONE GUTHRIE ACCEPTS STRATFORD BID TO ATTEND THIS YEAR'S FESTIVAL" was the headline of Herbert Whittaker's "Show Business" June 19 column in *The Globe and Mail* – the first of dozens of supportive articles which he would write over the following three decades.

"BRING AVON'S BARD TO OUR STRATFORD," demanded the heading of James Scott's "Book Talk" column in the Toronto *Telegram* also on June 19. "I can see no good reason why this big, prosperous and expanding land of ours could not attract some of the best talent in the world to tread Stratford's boards," he wrote. "We have a fine group of competent actors who could form the nucleus of the company. Why not bring in a few great names and directors, and, in time, I have no doubt at all that we would turn out our own Oliviers and Richardsons. A dream? Not on your life. This could be done within a year and mayhap it will."

The Stratford *Beacon-Herald* could always be counted on to be supportive in its own sweet, if misspelled fashion. In an article headed "NOTED PRODUCER TO VISIT STRATFORD SOON," it stated that "Mr. Guthrie has been associated with such noted thespians as Sir Laurence Olivier, Allister [sic]

Sim, Vivien Leigh, Alex [sic] Guinness, Charles Laughton and Michael Rodgrave [sic]."

In his last letter to me before he arrived, dated June 24, 1951, Tyrone Guthrie underlined his hope that this would be "a *community* festival – not just a jamboree got up by a few arty types. The performances, in my opinion, should be professional to the last degree, but closely integrated in every way we can manage to the widest possible X-section of the community."

Followers of the history of the Stratford Festival, as well as lovers of Canadian literature, may be charmed to read one paragraph in Guthrie's hand-written letter: "I wonder if you are in touch with my friend Robertson Davies, c/o Peterborough Examiner, P'boro, Ont. He & his wife are ex-Old Vic people (she was a v. capable stage manager & he was laid on as a kind of resident pedant-cum-small-part-actor – he'd just left Oxford then – this is before the war). They are knowledgeable, madly keen and *very sensible*." More than sensible, as far as I and the eventual project were concerned – it was Robertson Davies who, in 1953, co-authored with Tyrone Guthrie the wonderful, laudatory book on the Festival, *Renown at Stratford*.

While Guthrie got his affairs in order back in Ireland and England, there were a number of organizational changes in responsibility for the Festival planning. Most important, an independent committee took over running the Festival from the City Council. The latter never formally announced "We're getting out of this"; it just happened.

Several months before the City Council gave me that generous $125 to sponsor my trip to New York to bag Sir Laurence Olivier, a man named Stan Blowes had suggested to the Chamber of Commerce that we "do something" about Stratford's Shakespeare connection. Blowes's idea was that we should have troubadors wandering through the park, singing Shakespearean songs and wearing Elizabethan costumes. He was a bit of a maverick, so the Chamber of Commerce punished him by making him chairman of a committee to investigate the idea. This group was not specifically dedicated to my Festival concept – indeed, I had not yet proposed it officially – it was merely out to "use" Shakespeare in some fashion or other.

I can not give an exact date, but at some point that spring it became clear that this Chamber of Commerce committee had taken over the Festival project from the City Council. Not that I was ever properly informed of the changeover. But, in retrospect, it was handy that this committee on "minstrels in the park" was around to take over the obligations of planning the Festival from the Chamber of Commerce. It was this committee (Stan Bowles was no longer chairman) that eventually evolved into the Stratford Shakespearean Festival Foundation.

The committee was soon enlarged by other people I brought into it, so it became much more important. Of course, *anything* would be more important than a committee originally set up to announce, "Okay, go out and get yourself a lute player who will wander through the park."

Who were some of the men and women who helped create the Stratford Festival as much as I ever did? Who were the people who were willing to meet three, four, even five times a week for hours each time, on a volunteer basis, from June 1952 through to the start of the Festival in the summer of 1953 – and beyond?

Here are some of the major faces and forces on that committee, who later became members of the board of the Stratford Shakespearean Festival Foundation.

Alan Skinner, a doctor from London, Ontario, who was very involved with that city's Little Theatre.

Robertson Davies, who joined the board because of his love of Shakespearean theatre, and because of his long and warm friendship with Tyrone Guthrie. He was the editor of the Peterborough *Examiner* at the time, but has more recently gained renown for such works as The Deptford Trilogy (*Fifth Business, World of Wonders*, and *The Manticore*), *What's Bred In The Bone*, and much more. He came to all the important meetings of the Stratford board and was a great help and source of strength.

Al Knight, a Stratford industrialist, and a good, solid worker with, thank God, a wry sense of humour.

Judge Harold Lang of the Perth County Court, a decent fellow who came regularly to all meetings.

Charles Isard, another Londoner and faithful member.

William Kalbfleisch, the manager of the Stratford branch of the Bank of Montreal. His competency is suggested by his appointment, in later years, as a vice-president of that very major bank, after serving in Vancouver as head of their Western division. I have no doubt – nor do I regret it for an instant – that his career was advanced greatly by the many contacts he made while serving so ably on the Stratford board. It was he who served as Treasurer for the Festival, often crawling very far out on a limb because of the money the bank had advanced us. (One more of life's many ironies: Banks loan tens of millions to South American dictatorships, but balk at loaning a few thousand to a non-profit, Canadian cultural organization. And unlike the South American countries, we managed to pay them back.)

Ken Crone, the head of the Stratford branch of the London Life Insurance.

Walter Barlow, from the small, neighbouring town of Woodstock, whose football team always managed to wallop ours. He was a very good member of the board and was involved in the Little Theatre in his town.

The Venerable Archdeacon F.G. Lightbourne of the St. James Anglican Church, who was always a great help. He lent a certain dignity to an organization which often needed it. A major leader in the Stratford Ministerial Association, he welcomed Alec Guinness into his home, where he stayed that first, very special summer.

Norm Kaye, the manager of the Silverwood Dairy in Stratford, and a very good worker. He also headed the Chamber of Commerce and later became the president of the Stratford Festival. It was he whom I went to when the City told me to meet with the Chamber of Commerce. He eventually went on to become one of the heads of the gigantic international company Weston, and was (and is) a great guy.

Jim Preston, the head of Preston Noelting, which manufactured office furniture, and another strong member.

John Penistan, the pathologist at the Stratford General

Hospital, an Englishman who had not lost his very British accent.

Mrs. Gordon (Ina) Honsberger, from Kitchener, who was involved with that city's Little Theatre. She was an admirable member and helped raise considerable sums of money in her city, which is less than thirty miles from Stratford. A homemaker, she was more than competent on the board.

Alf Bell, the vice-president of the Festival, and the president of Sealed Power Piston Rings. He worked like a horse. His wife, Dama, later joined the board.

Mrs. E.N.T. (Helen) Griffith, the wife of one of the wealthiest industrialists in the city. Her husband, Slim, surprised us all by assiduously planting shrubbery around the theatre's tent on opening day. Both of them were superb at fundraising.

Beth Hall, the secretary to the British Mortgage and Trust Corporation and a widow. Her husband had been a good friend of my late brother and was also killed during the war. Beth was a goldmine of support and common sense. She was also a member of the board who accompanied me and others to the U.S.S.R. during our official visit to that country in 1958. It was she who, in May 1953, when we were in the middle of our greatest financial crisis, began complaining about the number of minutes being taken, declaring, "It doesn't matter. It's going to flop anyway." I still do not know if she was being tongue-in-cheek.

Mrs. John Anderson, a homemaker, and the wife of a lawyer. It was her husband who drew up the charter for our non-profit Festival Foundation, and it is a source of pride to me that it has since been used in law books as a model charter of its kind.

In the second year of the Festival, at a major meeting with Tyrone Guthrie, the director recommended something the exact opposite of a recommendation he had made many months before. Mrs. Anderson – fearless as always – stood up and announced, "But Tony, that's *not* what you recommended last year!" Guthrie replied, quietly, "Oh? Well, I changed my mind!" She was the only one on the board with the courage to challenge him, and Tony admired that.

W.A. (Bill) Johnston, the president of a manufacturing

business. His wife would become the first actress from the town of Stratford to grace our Festival stage.

And finally, the indefatigable Dr. Harry Showalter, the president of the Stratford Festival board. His doctorate in chemistry and his ownership of the Kist Bottling Works (very soft drinks, alas) hardly explains his brilliance as our (elected) president. I recall one time, early on – perhaps in November 1952 – Harry came around to my mother's home, where I often stayed, to deliver the minutes of a meeting. He was bubbling with enthusiasm. When he left, my mother looked at me and declared, "If you've got Harry behind this Festival, and he likes it, he'll stay with you all the way. He's like a bulldog and won't let go." How right she was.

It still stuns and amazes me, over a third of a century later, how nearly every one of these very impressive people showed up, day after day, week after week. Without them, there would have been no Stratford Festival; of this, there can be no question.

Like a bureaucratic Topsy, the new committee just evolved. This committee was still under the official aegis of the Chamber of Commerce, which had many members who were not interested in a Shakespearean Festival. They wanted to get industry into the town, or better lighting, or whatever.

The meeting to discuss "the proposed Shakespearean Festival," was held in the board room of city hall on the evening of Tuesday, June 24, 1952. We discussed the coming visit of Tyrone Guthrie and such topics as our initial fundraising campaign ("Objective: $2,000"). The minutes of the meeting have the warmth and charm of a small-town picnic agenda:

1. Mr. Bob Beatty [retired Chief of Police – the one who allowed me in the jail during the Depression to research my "Tramps, Hobos, and Bums" project] might act as Mr. Guthrie's driver.
2. Miss Shirley Cox [daughter of Alderman Fred Cox, who arranged my first City Council meeting] might do secretarial work for him.
3. It might be advisable to inform Mr. Guthrie of existing

facilities in the Park so that he would not make plans that would conflict with them.

4. Mr.Guthrie's visit should be kept as informal as possible.
5. Dr. Showalter asked that the members of the committee be on call during Mr. Guthrie's visit.

In a letter to me, Tyrone Guthrie had written that "You'll be able to pick me out, because I'll be the tallest one getting off the plane." I, in turn, described myself as being bald, and told him I would be wearing a bow-tie. As his plane was due late that evening, he was to stay at Dora Mavor Moore's home the first night. Dora and I had planned to meet him, but, on the night, she could not get dressed fast enough, and felt obliged to stay behind to tidy the house for him. She was in a real state. So I finally took off on my own and went out to the old Malton airport, northwest of Toronto – a terrible place.

I stood there waiting for Guthrie's plane to come in. He had flown from England to Montreal and then had caught a local flight to Toronto. As fortune (and men's eyes) would have it, there had been some kind of gathering of the RCMP in Montreal, and everybody who got off his plane was six foot four and taller!

I began to panic because all the passengers were so huge. On top of it all, Guthrie had a haircut like these men as well. (Bruce West later described the director as looking like a policeman. Guthrie, like Queen Victoria, was not amused.)

Finally, I spotted this big, tall fellow standing in the lobby looking kind of lost. I noticed that he (fortunately) had a briefcase. So I strolled around him until I spotted the initials "T.G." on it.

"Excuse me. Are you Tyrone Guthrie?" I asked.

"Yes," he replied. "And you must be Tom Patterson."

Shakespeare would have written a better exchange, but it served the purpose. We went off together in my car and immediately started to talk about the Festival. We were so engrossed, I lost my way to Dora's house. We drove around quite a bit before we finally arrived.

"Oh my God!" cried the director, suddenly. In our excitement, we had left his luggage at the airport! A number of calls later, we located it and had it delivered the next day. But luggage be damned. I was so very, very impressed with the great director! I knew by his probing questions that he was just as excited as I by the idea of the Festival and was obviously keen to get involved. Furthermore, he was fully aware of how non-existent our funds were.

That first night, Dora Mavor Moore, Tyrone Guthrie, I, and committee chairman Harry Showalter, who had driven into Toronto to meet the director, stayed up until three, maybe even four that morning, talking endlessly about theatre. The next morning, luggage firmly in hand, we drove to Stratford.

On the way to my home town, we stopped in the city of Guelph for something to eat. Back in the early 1950s, Ontario was dry (and I don't mean low rainfall). While we were giving our order to the waitress, she asked all of us if we wanted "something to drink?" Guthrie looked up at the young woman and said, "Scotch."

The waitress was speechless, since to drink liquor in a restaurant in those days was unheard of. (When the Scotsman/Irishman learned that "to drink" in an Ontario restaurant meant tea, coffee, milk, or orange juice, it amused him mightily.)

When we got to Stratford, it looked pretty dreary – not like it does today. I decided not to take him straight down Ontario Street; first impressions are so important. So I turned to him and announced, "Tony, I'm going to take you to see the theatre site right away!"

We headed down along River Drive, and got out at the island. We stood on a rise of grass, below where the theatre sits today.

"You see? That's where we would like the theatre," I told him.

Guthrie looked at the grassy area, and then he looked around and saw the island. As I quickly learned, he was crazy about water, almost like a child running through ocean waves.

"Why don't we do it here? We can do it on barges. And where that bridge is – we can widen that part of the river. Then we'll have the backstage on the other side of the island, and have the different scenes on the barges and come around.

The audience can be over here, where the parking lot is now."

His reverie continued, about a revolving stage and barges going back and forth. ". . .and we can have the seats over here, and the parking can be down there." He abruptly stopped and thought better about it. "No. It won't work. I guess up there is better."

It was fun to watch him think. He would go to the nth degree with an idea that you or I might think was crazy from the start. But he would follow it right through to the end before he concluded that "it won't work."

I was not about to tell him at that time that the land that we were looking at had not been put aside, and that it was not ours for building upon. As I was to discover later, nobody really knew who owned the park. Part of it apparently belonged to the Stratford Parks Board, and part of it was owned by the provincial government of Ontario. But there had never been a proper survey of the boundary.

But that was not the immediate concern of Tyrone Guthrie, famed theatre director from England. Since the 1930s, he had been the leader of a movement in Great Britain that wanted to stage Shakespeare the way that the Bard had written the plays for. Even before the war, when he was directing at Stratford, England, Guthrie built an apron out over the orchestra pit so that the stage projected somewhat into the audience, a bit of a thrust. But he realized that it still did not work, because behind the proscenium you are working, visually, in two dimensions, while in front of it, you are working in three.

After the war, Rudolf Byng invited Guthrie to direct the drama for the new Edinburgh Festival, which Byng was starting. They shopped around for a theatre. Tony, of course, was looking for a likely site for an apron stage. At the time, he showed the kind of persuasiveness that would prove to be so important to the Stratford Festival in Ontario. He managed to convince the elders of the Church of Scotland that they should change their Assembly Hall – almost the Vatican of the Presbyterian Church – into a theatre!

This hall is built much like a small House of Commons. Down its centre is a table – a huge, old table that was built to be there for eternity. Along each side of it are large, wooden seats, like thrones, with high backs. At the head of this table, where the moderator sits, is a kind of old Scottish throne, quite Jacobean. All these chairs were permanently attached to the floor. On three sides of the table and chairs are pews, much like the seats in the House of Commons.

The Church of Scotland agreed to lend Guthrie their hall for a theatre on one condition: He could not move the table, chairs, or throne. So the stage had to be built high over the top of the lot, which left no room for a backstage, and no proscenium at all. It was a rough and ready apron stage. The steps coming down from the main stage into what we call the gutter were perhaps six inches wide and a foot high. The entrances were from under the stage – the performers had to crawl underneath through the legs of the table and chairs, to make their entrance.

When Guthrie arrived in Stratford, he was still dreaming of creating a theatre with an apron stage and, in Stratford, he realized he had found his opportunity. He saw this lovely piece of grass on which he could achieve the culmination of all his experimental work at the original Stratford and at the Edinburgh Festival.

Here, it could be done! Here, he had nobody to set conditions beforehand. When he later suggested his highly original concept for the stage, the committee accepted it, not knowing that it was so revolutionary. They said, "If Tony wants it, then fine; we'll do it."

After Guthrie had taken a good look at the proposed site for the theatre, we drove to my mother's house, where Guthrie was to give his first press conference. We used my mother's house for the conference as we could not afford to rent a hotel room large enough to contain all the reporters who had arrived.

Guthrie had had a rough few days. He had flown in from England; he had been up for most of the previous night talking with Dora, Harry, and myself; and he had just driven in from Toronto. There was a lot of "this goddam thing will never work" in the air, along with whisperings from the Toronto press of "who's going to drive from Toronto to Stratford to see Shakespeare?" (A nemesis of mine had written the first of many letters to the editor of *The Beacon-Herald* the day before, asking "Are there signs, anywhere, that the public has a great unsatisfied hunger for performances of Shakespeare's plays? I doubt it. . . .Do we *have* to have a Shakespeare festival? After all, this is Stratford, Canada, not Stratford, England.")

Tyrone Guthrie came down from his room late – he may have been napping – and at first the reporters were surly. "How do you expect people to come all the way from Toronto to Stratford?" one asked him. Guthrie replied, "Look at the number of people who come all the way from Canada to Stratford-on-Avon, England!" He absolutely wowed them. The press found the lanky Scot/Irishman genial, bright, and witty. "The festival in your Stratford could be better [than its British counterpart]," he told them. "Shakespeare could be presented on a stage that would reproduce the intimate actor-audience relation for which he wrote. Indeed, here in Canada, you could have the finest Shakespearean productions in the world."

Guthrie drummed away at his idea for a stage that would be "built out into the theatre, so that people almost surround the stage. It means returning to the old style of acting, in which gestures are less grotesque, and less scenery is required. The audience is able more to feel a part of the proceedings."

He knew enough to praise the citizens of Stratford: "Seldom have I come into a community which shows so much enthusiasm for a project labelled mad." But, he went on, "the scheme is not so crazy. However, it is not a means of making money, and cannot be. If you want to make money, I suggest musical comedy shows, with plenty of girls and nice tunes. [As I recall, Tony called them Girlie-Girlie Shows.] But if efficiently run, the scheme is not a money-losing proposition." Guthrie explained that "other assets more than make up for [box office deficits]. There is world-wide publicity. The festival at Edinburgh calls attention not only to that city but also to Scotland and its lesser appendages, England and Wales." (That comment got a great laugh.)

The director charmed the press – and, later that same day,

the members of the recently created Shakespearean Festival committee – with an anecdote about how "the moment a Briton sets foot in Canada, he feels the bustle and excitement of boom days." He recalled what he saw at the Montreal airport, just the day before. American passengers were going into the airport restaurant for food, and putting down "twenty- and fifty-dollar bills" to pay for it. "The little French-Canadian cashier calmly returned their change, less four cents on each dollar, leading to howls of anguish from the U.S. visitors." Laughed Guthrie, "But that little cashier remained calm and unperturbed. In her fetching accent and with ice-cold politeness, she explained the economics of the Canadian dollar, and kept right on deducting four cents from the U.S. dollar." This, suggested the director, was a significant vignette of Canada's material wealth – real and potential.

I recall only one really bad moment at that press conference. Tony kept referring to "Stratters-on-Avon" and "Stratters, Canada" in a rather disarming, slang way. An alderman, Fred Cox, leaped up and demanded, "It's *Stratford*," not *Stratters*!" Guthrie pulled in his horns and apologized.

Guthrie's scrawled notes for his first meeting with the committee later that day are preserved in the Stratford Festival Archives:

RESULTS IN THE CATEGORY OF REMAINING TO BE SEEN.
   COULD SUCCEED, COULD FAIL: PROBABLY ELEMENTS OF BOTH.
LOOK AT GLOOMY SIDE FIRST: LOSS OF MONEY. LOSS OF FACE.
LOSS OF FACE: TRIED TO DO SOMETHING INTELLIGENT.
   1. SHAKESPEARE PLAYS.
   2.   "   STAGE.
   3. CANADIAN ACTORS
   4. OUTSIDE HELP
   5. BOLD SCALE
LOSS OF MONEY: IF IT WAS SOMETHING INTELLIGENT
THEN LOSS OF MONEY OK
COMPARABLE TO A MINING OPERATION.
        "   "   SCHOLARSHIP.
IF SUCCESSFUL

1. DEMONSTRATION OF MATURITY
   ART IS IMPORTANT
2. TECHNICAL DEMONSTRATION OF LASTING IMPORTANCE
3. CANADIANS STAY IN CANADA,
4. TRIUMPHANT ACT OF FAITH.
   WAKE UP TO BARD RALLY.

Perhaps even more important than the impression Tyrone Guthrie made on the press and the people of Stratford, was the way the latter impressed Tyrone Guthrie. As he humorously described in his autobiography, *A Life in the Theatre*:

> In the course of thirty years I have had experience of many sorts of committees and boards who manage theatrical enterprises. I expected that this one would consist mainly of artistic and excitable elderly ladies of both sexes, with a sprinkling of businessmen to restrain the artistic people from spending money. There would also be an anxious nonentity from the Town Hall, briefed to see that no municipal funds were promised, but also to see that, if any success were achieved, the municipality would get plenty of credit. The point about this sort of committee is that the artistic ones have extremely definite views, but so conflicting that it is easy for a tiny minority of businessmen to divide and conquer. Prudent, sensible, businesslike counsel prevails. The result is that nothing whatsoever gets done. In Britain the average age of members is seventy-three.

What Guthrie discovered, in my native town, was something quite different indeed:

> My first surprise at Stratford, therefore, was to find that most members of the committee were quite young. I was almost the oldest person present. The second surprise was to find that the males outnumbered the females by about five to one. The women spoke seldom, but when they did their remarks were usually briefer and more practical than those of the men.

The greatest surprise was now to come. The committee was unanimous in wishing to organize a festival; it had given proof of this by raising a fund out of members' own pockets to get me out to give advice; now, instead of excited babble quickly turning to acrimonious dispute, there was a silence. They were waiting, with every appearance of interest, even of respect, for me to give my advice.

And advice is what Guthrie gave. He was stunned – and ecstatic – to find himself someplace where he did not have to fight traditionalists. There were no traditionalists because there was no theatre in Stratford, Ontario, to be traditional about. He was not troubled that committee members had no knowledge of theatre. Rather, he was relieved that they did not *pretend* that they had knowledge of theatre. I remember that he was actually shocked that no one fought him over his idea of an apron stage. "If you say that Shakespeare needs an apron stage," they told him, "then that's acceptable to us. Just get us a festival."

The above might make the committee look a little stupid, but they were not. This was clear from the kind of questions they asked Guthrie, especially (as he noted himself in his autobiography) those the women asked. I played an almost inactive part in the meeting, as I wanted the committee members to do the questioning, and to let Tony do the answering.

Their questions were pretty soul-searching. Not "what shows will we do?" nor "I remember when we did *Hamlet* back in high school." The women committee members asked questions such as "How much will this cost?"; "How many people will we have to have?"; "How long will it run each summer?"; to which he answered "It'll cost a lot"; "That's for you to decide," and "That's the business end of it."

Guthrie was pleased, as well, to encounter the attitude of the people of Stratford: business-like, small-town, but solid. And he was delighted that the committee did not want merely a tourist attraction.

He was aware that there was no money, but he was extremely impressed that the committee had raised the funds needed to get him out to Stratford. (When Harry Showalter had learned that Guthrie was definitely coming, he had assessed each member of the committee, phoned each one, and had insisted – he had not just asked them – "I want two hundred bucks from you"; "I need three hundred from you"; "You have to give one hundred," and so on. And he had received what he needed, one or two thousand dollars, the very next day).

Money would, of course, be a constant concern for the Stratford Festival, which is why Guthrie was also touched by the response to his declaration that "this thing is going to cost a lot of money" – nobody flinched. The committee was aware that the Festival would cost a great deal, and aware of what they were stepping into. That is what I mean when I say that they had good business sense. From their first meeting with Guthrie, they knew that this was not going to be a small, backyard affair.

After that fateful and most promising first meeting with the committee, which took place at Alf and Dama Bell's home, Dora Mavor Moore and I took the director back to where he was staying at the Windsor Hotel, now called 23 Albert Place. In our concern to introduce Guthrie to the press and to the committee, we had never checked him in! And here it was, two o'clock in the morning. There was absolutely nobody around, and I mean nobody.

"I'll get in" smiled Guthrie, who proceeded to walk behind the hotel desk and begin to fiddle with the cash register.

Like Pavlov's dog responding eagerly to a bell, a short, lame, roly-poly man, who had obviously been sleeping, stumbled in, looked up at this giant of a man towering over his cash register and nearly hit the roof.

We proceeded to calm the night watchman down, and then we checked Tony in, leaving him until the morning.

It was some days later that we found out that Guthrie had sat nearly until dawn with the night watchman talking about Stratford and its populace. But then, what better way to find out about a town and its inhabitants, especially a town where you might be working in the months and years ahead?

During his stay in Canada, a prestigious radio programme of the time, "Our Special Speaker," which followed the CBC "National News" on Sunday nights, contacted Tony Guthrie and invited him on the show. He agreed immediately, because he was anxious to do anything to promote the idea of the Festival.

On the day I drove him to the CBC radio studios in Toronto, he turned to me and said, "Tom, I'm pleased to do this. But I'm a professional, and I think that I should get a fee. I mean, we have to establish right off the top that this is a professional operation."

"I agree that you should get paid," I told him, "but I don't think that it'll be very much."

"That doesn't matter. It's the principle of the thing."

When we got to the radio building, we discussed the programme with the producer, and as we finished, Tony asked, "Now, what about a fee?"

"Mr. Guthrie," said the producer, "this is considered a prestige spot, and we usually give, if anything, an honorarium, which most people donate to their favourite charity."

"I don't care what you call it," insisted Guthrie. "What's the fee?"

The producer seemed to be getting very embarrassed, and he finally said, "We normally give twenty-five dollars."

"Doesn't sound like very much to me," declared the theatre director. "Let's make it fifty dollars."

"I think that we can manage that," said the producer. And that was that.

It was all part of Tyrone Guthrie's contribution to establishing the Stratford Festival as a professional theatre. If he was to take part in a radio programme, then he had to get the going fee, or better. It did not matter how much he was paid. If they had offered a thousand dollars he would have asked for two thousand. But they offered twenty-five dollars, so he asked for fifty.

The week that Guthrie left for Great Britain, papers across Canada printed the full transcript of his talk on "Our Special Speaker." I think that some of his key points are well worth reprinting here:

Is there a Canadian theatre? I don't know. I expect there is probably more going on than is heard of at long distance. But we have heard of Fridolin; we have heard of Les Compagnons; we know that in the Ontario summer there are seasons of stock with professional actors whose standard would be even higher than it is if they were not battling against the odds of unsuitable accommodation and inadequate time for rehearsal. Also we know there are the Little Theatres and the Dominion Drama Festival.

They have, I know, done good and even distinguished work – but in the amateur field. They have not so far been able to offer either a living wage, or – not less important – a full life's work to more than a tiny handful of people. Most of the gifted Canadian youngsters have to leave Canada and make their contribution to a theatre, whether in Europe or the United States, that has no real connection with their native land.

Canada has, I know, made a distinctive contribution on the dramatic side of radio, and may shortly do so in television; but these mechanized arts are not the theatre – they are an ersatz substitute. They bear the same relation to the theatre as a telephone conversation to real conversation – in fact, a poor relation. Semi-occasionally, Toronto is regarded by American impresarios as what is called a touring date – after all, it is cheaper to send a show to Toronto than to St. Louis or Kansas City.

What likelihood is there that there will be a more flourishing theatre in Canada? None, unless Canadians begin to feel that a serious theatre is not merely an amenity – a rather long-haired amenity principally for the use of rich women – but a necessity. Don't mistake me; naturally nobody thinks that the theatre is a necessity quite in the same category as bread. It is perfectly possible to live without any theatrical art as it is perfectly possible to live without being able to read. . . .

The theatre in Canada will not be able to make much headway unless Canadians are willing to judge it in terms of quality – not just in terms of success measured in cash. . . .

We must not make the mistake of thinking, in the theatre

any more than elsewhere, that the cash standard is final simply because it is assessable. By the way, I hope I haven't conveyed the impression that I'm one of those people who think that the theatre must all the time be intensely serious. Far from it. I believe that, in art as in life, the serious is, and should be, shot through with absurdity and fun. I like to think of the theatre as a place where the mighty are cast down and where the humble and meek are exalted, where serious people and ideas have their pants pulled off, but where – paradoxically – fun is deadly serious.

During his two-week visit to Canada, I took Tony to see a number of theatres. We visited Melody Fair, a theatre-in-the-round which was out in New Toronto somewhere. Tony was impressed with the in-the-round concept, especially by how it helped the audience get involved in the performance.

We then went to the Straw Hat Performance in Port Carling, organized by the famous Canadian theatrical family of the Davises – Donald, Murray, and their sister, Barbara Chilcott. As I had relatives in Port Carling, I was able to get tickets for the two of us privately, and neither the Davises nor the cast had any idea that Guthrie was in the audience. After the performance, Donald found out for whom they had been performing. He was furious. He has since forgiven me, I think, for not announcing our presence. Needless to say, Tony was very impressed with the talent displayed.

My wife ran a camp called Gay Venture near Minden, so we spent a weekend there before driving to Peterborough where Guthrie spent time with his old friend, Robertson Davies. On the trip from Port Carling to Minden, we discussed who might be the lead performers at our prospective Festival. We decided that we needed to find a good Shakespearean actor who would be recognized in North America. It was on this northern journey that we settled on Alec Guinness.

It was also on this trip that Tony first suggested we find a designer right away. I could not understand what the hurry was, not knowing anything about theatre. After all, we had not even chosen the plays yet. He also said that a woman named Tanya Moiseiwitsch was one of England's greatest designers, and we should try to get her. It did not matter to me that I had not heard of her; if Tony said she was the best, that was good enough. In retrospect, this shows the advantages of naïvety. (Admittedly, there are plenty of drawbacks, as well.) When people invite the leader of a field to give advice, they are probably safe to accept it. While this may seem axiomatic, I have since run into several cases where this did not occur. But in the case of Tanya, the choice of designer could not have been better. She proved to be a tower of strength under difficult circumstances, and still, after thirty-five years, provides continued strength and support as associate artistic director of the Festival.

During our drive back from our Cook's tour of Ontario culture, it was hot as hell. My car had plastic seats, we had the windows open, and the dust just poured into the car. Nylon shirts had recently become popular because they were washable, but Tony had brought only two such shirts with him for his two-week trip to Canada. We used to stop in gas stations, and he would go in and wash one shirt and then hang it in the car to dry.

We arrived back in Stratford with little time to spare before we were to meet again with the committee. We just had time for a quick bath at the Windsor Hotel. My guest had his bath first and then announced: "We haven't got very much time; you'd better use my water." I did so, and while I splashed about in his bath water, he went to the basin to wash his dirty shirt. All of a sudden I heard, "Jesus Christ!" He had washed the wrong shirt!

"Well," Tony said. "This is a big meeting, and it's formal. I'd better wear my suit."

So Guthrie put on his black suit, which made him look more like a cop than ever, and wore his dirty shirt because the clean one was wet.

The committee meeting was in the Stratford city hall, and it was a very hot night. Everyone there was in shirtsleeves, so Tony said "Oh, to hell with it!" and took off his coat. He now stood there in a shirt that was absolutely filthy with dust, with his suspenders showing, and made his recommendations from notes jotted down on the back of a Sweet Caporal cigarette package. His informality broke down a lot of barriers with the locals who were present, and I suspect that he took off his jacket for that psychological reason as much as because he was a lot cooler without it.

Before this gathering took place, Tony and I had talked about our next move. "I can't tell them to send *you* to London," he said. "But I've got to recommend that *somebody* be sent to London." As it turned out, it was I who went on the mission to track down our major performer. As Guthrie told the committee that night, "We need a star. And as far as Shakespeare is concerned, the only stars are in England." (I often wonder to this day whether Tony was aware of some subtle tensions or divisiveness already surfacing in the committee, which he was consciously trying to alleviate by not specifically recommending me to make the trip to find the star. But, it is nice to report, no one else was considered for the journey.)

It was at this time, as well, that we had a lengthy discussion about the tent. He had been to Melody Fair, which was a theatre-in-the-round in a tent – a summer operation that brought in stars for such productions as *Oklahoma!* Tony was not particularly impressed with the performance that night, but he was enthused by the possibilities of the tent.

When he made his recommendations, he stated, "Now, you won't be able to raise the money for a building, but I saw a tent operation in Toronto which I rather liked. Why don't you go ahead and build the stage, and then put a tent over the top of it?"

But for all his practicality, when it came to what happens on a stage, it had to be right, no matter the cost. Only then would he look at ways to cut down expenses. He was involved in fundraising from the very beginning and always aware of our financial needs. When we were in a panic during later financial crises, he kept himself well informed.

That last meeting before Guthrie returned to England was quite dramatic, because two people on the committee abruptly resigned. One of them was an accountant, who felt that "this thing is getting out of hand." The other was the publisher of the local paper, *The Beacon-Herald*, who simply stood up, resigned right in front of Guthrie, and left the room. (I later found out that the publisher was having difficulties with his business at the time, and that the

Thomson chain was in town that very day, trying to buy his newspaper. He was frightened to get involved in this additional project, so he pulled out).

The resignations were quite a shock – it felt to me as if the whole project had fallen apart – but, in a way, it strengthened Guthrie's resolve to believe in the remaining members. The resignations of these two fairly important citizens gave room for others – if they were weak – to declare, "Maybe we'd better have second thoughts about this, too."

This did not happen. Instead, those who witnessed the resignations passed a recommendation – with no money raised at all – to send me to England. It was unbelievably brave of them. They were quite aware of the commitment they were making, and they knew full well that this would be no church-basement theatre production; it was a major project.

Guthrie himself was unable to discuss actual figures, because he had no idea about costs of things in Canada. But he most definitely put the onus on the committee to raise the money and get the star. At one point at that final meeting, someone asked, quite casually, "Couldn't you do that for us?"

"No," he replied firmly. "I'm not going to be your agent. If you are going to do this festival, then it has to be you who makes the approach. I will not make the approach to anybody in England."

So the money-raising and star-getting was up to us. In essence, he was saying, "This is what you've got to do. If you want to do it, you've got to raise the money."

The issue of money also came up on Guthrie's last day in Stratford. We had agreed to pay him a $500 fee, but we had to settle up expenses, as well. The chairman of the committee, Harry Showalter, was also superintendent of the local Baptist Sunday School, and he neither drank, swore, nor smoked. His favourite reading was the two great English works, the King James Version of the Bible, and the plays of Shakespeare. Showalter had accepted Guthrie's fee for advising us on the festival, but he was determined not to let anyone else but himself negotiate the expenses of this theatrical fellow.

When we met for the final time in Stratford that July, we stood in front of my mother's house. Guthrie was a good six foot four inches and Harry Showalter at five foot six stared up at the visitor like a little bantam.

"All right now," Showalter said, with some passion, expecting a huge sum and a fight to match. "Come on. This expense thing. How much?" (We had taken care of Guthrie's hotel bill and all his meals, but there were still other expenses.)

"I tell you, how about five dollars?" smiled Guthrie.

Harry Showalter was absolutely flabbergasted. "Come, come! It *must* be more than that!"

"I know that you haven't got any money," said Tony, "and I've had a marvellous time. You've looked after me well, and I've been well fed. So five dollars is fine."

"Come," cried Showalter, suddenly generous. "It *must* be more than that! We'll make it ten!"

Guthrie reached down to pat his host on the shoulder, "Tell you what, Harry. How about splitting the difference? We'll make it seven fifty."

Tyrone Guthrie received seven dollars and fifty cents for expenses and went back to Ireland.

6

My Conquest of England

In September 1952, my mother, my wife, and I flew to Edinburgh, Scotland, to see a Guthrie production of *Romeo and Juliet*. Tony felt that it would be a good idea if I saw his festival there, and we loved it. Then, while the two women in my life stayed to enjoy the rest of the Scottish Festival, I headed off to London to meet with Sir Michael Balcon, the international head of J. Arthur Rank Productions, which handled most of Alec Guinness's film work. Balcon, in turn, set up a meeting with the fine English actor. (My boss at Maclean Hunter, Floyd Chalmers, had put me in touch with Balcon. It certainly pays to know people in high places.)

My dreams of obtaining Alec Guinness were by no means assured, however. True, Tyrone Guthrie was the godfather of the actor's son, and they were very close friends. But would Guinness be available, and could we afford him?

Of the former, there was considerable question. From January through June 1950, Guinness had been the talk of Broadway with his appearance as Sir Henry Harcourt-Reilly, the metaphysical psychiatrist in T.S. Eliot's verse drama, *The Cocktail Party*. When *The Sunday Times* theatre critic, Harold Hobson, saw him in the role at Brighton, he declared that "Mr. Guinness is going to be one of our greatest actors. The triangle of Gielgud, Olivier, and Richardson is visibly changing into a quadrilateral." True, Guinness had done a *Hamlet* which was considered a bomb, but I had no idea how important that one failure would be to my quest. As early as 1945, Guinness had adapted *Great Expectations* for the screen, and played the role of Herbert Pocket; he had performed as Fagin in the film version of *Oliver Twist* in 1949, and had played all eight heirs to a dukedom in the film *Kind Hearts and Coronets*, displaying a comic genius as well.

Because of Guthrie's close relationship with Guinness, we in Stratford thought that he would talk to the actor on his return to England. But no such luck – it was up to us to negotiate with the star. Guthrie made this point absolutely clear by not returning to England, but, instead, to his ancestral home in Ireland. In Annagh-ma Kerrig there would be no chance of his running into Guinness and of having to discuss the project with him.

So there I was, forced to confront the fine actor myself, and in a most intimidating place. Our initial meeting took place in his dressing room, in the West End theatre where Guinness was starring in *Under the Sycamore Tree*. It was the first time I had ever been backstage in a theatre, and to be ushered into the star's private room was a thrill. Indeed, I think I was more excited to be backstage, just before a performance, than I was to be talking with a star I had seen in many films. "What's he going to be like?" and "How should one act backstage?" were but two of the questions which were swirling in my mind.

Luckily for me, Alec Guinness was very charming and immediately put me at ease. He poured me a drink, and we began to chat. Then he started to put on his make-up for that evening's performance, and we began discussing the prospective Festival. I was sitting on a small sofa in one corner of the room, and he was in the other corner, facing his mirror, with his back to me.

It was very disconcerting to discover that he could see my reflection in his mirror, but that I had no way of seeing his reactions to what I had to say. And in the middle of my spiel, the phone rang. It was his agent, wanting him to accept a film in Hollywood. My heart sank: There goes our chance, I thought. And had not Guthrie told the Stratford board, at the July 22, 1952 meeting, that "if 'stars' of inter-national calibre are available, [he] would anticipate small difficulty in financing the project?" But I was relieved to hear Guinness turn the offer down in no uncertain terms, saying that he thought he would have other commitments. I prayed that one of them might be Stratford! I later learned that, although the actor was under contract to Rank, he could accept other work if he desired. It was a Hollywood film, not a Rank one, which he had just rejected.

Guinness finally agreed to think about my proposal, and we made another appointment to meet the following night, once again in his dressing room. For the next twenty-four hours, my wife and my mother (who had accompanied me to England at their own expense; federal politicians take note!) joined in my mood of terrified exhilaration. Once again, my incurable optimism came to the fore; after that first meeting I was *sure* we had him.

It did not take long at our second meeting for my feeling to be justified. In his very quiet way, and with that famous Guinness grin, he said, "Yes, I will come." I doubt if he knew that he was not only changing my life with his decision, but also, as it turned out, changing the history of a town he had never heard of before then, and even the theatrical scene of an entire country.

But his generous agreement presented a problem. Up until this time, money had never been mentioned, and frankly, I had no idea how to broach the subject. So I continued to talk about other things. I suggested that he talk to Guthrie and get his reaction, to which he also agreed.

Finally, I was forced to start talking about remuneration.

"We, uh, we will not be able to pay you the commercial fee you could get from films or the West End, but we would like you to bring your family out and make your visit into a holiday. And your son could go to my wife's camp, in Haliburton!"

At this point, Guinness turned away from his make-up mirror, stared at me, and said firmly, "Don't talk that way with me, or anyone else in England. You are going to lose money on this project, so don't go around offering all these goodies!" (What goodies? I thought to myself. A summer-camp experience for his child?)

I was greatly relieved to hear the call boy crying "LAST CALL," so I quickly made my exit. Before I left, I arranged a luncheon meeting for the next day, after he had spoken with Tony Guthrie.

On the way back to the hotel where my mother and wife were ensconced and waiting, the size of the problem really struck home. Here we were, three Canadians, who had no experience of show business, with no money behind us, and no authorization to make an offer, discussing a contract with one of the hottest international stars in the business!

"What the hell do we pay him?" I asked them, in terror. I knew that anything I could offer him would have nothing to do with reality. Furthermore, I had to try to figure out how much we could afford, as I was determined not to go back to the committee in Stratford and present them with a sum that would scare the collective pants off them. I finally came up with the very un-Hollywood-like fee of $3,500.

The next day, Alec Guinness and I sat in a London restaurant discussing the festival. Right off the top, the actor said to me, "Oh! I got a letter from Guthrie!" And he pulled it out of his pocket and tossed it over to me.

It must have been a dozen pages long, in an envelope an inch thick. It was all hand-written, so I could not read it at a glance.

"Thank you very much!" I exclaimed, and shoved it into my pocket, where it quickly burned a hole. What had Guthrie told him?

"Can we talk money?" I finally asked Guinness. "We don't know what to offer you. We certainly do know that we can't give you what you are getting on a film or in the commercial theatre. . . .

"You know," I blurted out. "If this is stupid, just tell me, and it will go no further, and we'll see if we can come up with something else. How does thirty-five hundred sound?" I did not know – nor did Guinness – how long a period of time this would cover, nor how many plays he would be doing; I just knew that we needed him, and badly.

Guinness pulled a piece of paper from his pocket, along with a pencil, and calculated how much would be left of this sum after tax.

"Yes, that'll be fine." He paused for a moment and then added, "But I must make this one demand, Tom. I hope you understand and won't feel badly, but I must get at least a hundred dollars more than anyone else in the company."

I readily agreed. If he was to be the top man in the show, and this differential established him as such, then it was certainly acceptable to me.

So I had one of the finest actors of the middle of the twentieth century, for a little over a thousand dollars a month! He would not be earning as much money as the local conductor of our orchestra, back in Stratford, Ontario. (He ended up spending far more than he earned on such things as parties for his fellow performers that first summer. Indeed, after the Festival, Guinness even took back two young Canadian actors to England with him, put them up in his home, paid for them to attend a theatre school, and even helped them land positions in a West End production! One of the men was Richard Easton; the other is better known today as the author of some of the best Canadian novels ever written, including *The Wars* and *Famous Last Words* – Timothy Findley.)

Before I reached a final agreement with Guinness, there was one twelve-hour period of horror. Guinness and I agreed to meet in Tony Guthrie's London flat some days later. When I walked in, around six that evening, both men had already arrived. The atmosphere was icy.

"Alec changed his mind," Tony informed me. "He's not coming." I did not know that they had been quarrelling over that disastrous *Hamlet* of Guinness's from a number of years before.

I looked over to Guinness, who was sinking lower and lower into his chair. The famous actor was looking more and more like the "little man" he had played so brilliantly in the movies.

"Your reputation is *making* stars!" blurted out Guinness. "Once they *become* stars, you want nothing to do with them!"

Guthrie went white.

Then Guinness announced that he had to go to his evening performance. Guthrie did not even see him to the door as a proper host should. I guided the actor outside, murmuring to him, "I don't know what is going on here, but I would really like to see you again. Could we have lunch tomorrow?"

Just as Guinness was walking away, I added, "Yes, we *did* want a star, Alec. But it would have been easier and cheaper to go to New York. You see, we wanted a star who was also a classical actor." (In retrospect, it would have been far more costly to have hired a star from New York City. What American actor would have worked at Stratford, Ontario for many months, for $250 a week? But I was sincere in my words at the time.)

When I returned to the room, Guthrie started cursing.

"He's right, dammit! I HATE stars!!"

The next afternoon, at our lunch, Guinness apologized for the quarrel he had had with Guthrie, saying that was over which plays they might do at the Festival at Stratford. The implication was that he was reluctant to do the one about the melancholy Dane, his nemesis play.

"Shakespeare wrote more than one or two plays," I grinned. By the time lunch was over, Guinness again agreed to join our promising Festival.

In the archives of the Stratford Festival there sits a typewritten copy of the letter Tony Guthrie wrote to Alec Guinness in September 1952, which had burned such a large hole in my jacket pocket during our meeting in that London restaurant. This Epistle to the Briton gives a striking insight into how modest Guthrie was, and just how much faith he had in our (cashless) Shakespearean project even at that very early date:

My dear Alec,

The telephone is hopeless. Even when one can hear better than this morning, I think it is so hard to collect one's thoughts and talk sense.

The Canadian plan: you may think it a bit odd that I didn't get in touch with you when I got back from Canada. Refrained from doing so purposely: i) thought it more suitable that the first approach should be "official" from the Committee; ii) was very anxious that you (or any other leading actor) should feel free to discuss another director than yours truly if it seemed a better idea. Nothing is more tiresome than to be offered something and then find an unacceptable personality is bundled up in the package.

With you and me this situation would be the more troublesome because we are old friends.

Now, however, that you have been "officially" approached and are "interested" and also interested in my co-operation, I feel entirely free to discuss:

(a) Committee – I met them as you probably know, several times at Stratford. Had expected to find a typical hick town committee of dull trades persons led by the nose by one or two madly enthusiastic cranks. Not at all. They were extremely intelligent, realistic and – most surprising of all – humble. They realize that they don't know all about it; and are prepared to be guided, provided they feel confident that the guiding is responsible.

(b) Finance – This, I am convinced, will not be hard to find. Your name will guarantee that the project is not just a small-town jamboree. They (the committee) wish to finance and put this over in a big way. I think they can. We must discuss other safeguards – not merely of our own salaries – but to ensure that we are only embroiled in the project if it is being tackled as a matter of more than merely local interest and that, if it fails, it is not on account of parsimony.

I consider the fact that they were willing to pay me to go out and give advice; and then to pay for Tom to come over on their behalf and take the first steps to implement that advice, augurs well for the fact that the project will not be undertaken in a niggardly manner.

(c) Tent – my idea to build would be madness before the idea has been proved seaworthy. Shakespeare, out of doors, I'm sure you agree, is utterly impossible. The tent can look very beautiful and interesting (I have strong hopes that we can get Tanya to undertake the decor for the scheme) and inside it one can put the practicalities of an Elizabethan stage. Saw a musical comedy in Toronto in a tent (not well arranged) and acoustics were not bad at all.

I feel after my grapples in Edinboro with the Assembly

Hall, and especially after seeing *Romeo and Juliet* there, that the audience all around the actors is the *only way* with Swan of Avon.

(d) Broader Aspects – what interests me particularly about this is that I'm convinced it's the *right moment*. If Stratford doesn't do it, some other Canadian community will. Canada's bursting with money and, more important, Canada asks *us* (I mean "us" as Europeans, and, more particularly, as denizens of the Old Country) to help. And very, very important that we offer our help tactfully and responsibly.

In my opinion we must not try to annex the project and use it for our own private advancement. If it advances us, it must be part of a larger and more significant advancement. I know you'll agree about this.

And I *hope* you'll also agree about this: it should demonstrably be a Canadian scheme carried through by Canadians, but with help (indispensable and important help) from Great Britain.

Canada is likely in a surprisingly few years to be the richest and most powerful country in the world. There is a great sentimental urge in Canada to be influenced by Britain. There is a great practical urge to be influenced by the U.S.A. . . .almost every common sense argument based upon geography and economics drives Canada and the U.S.A. into one another's arms.

If we (the British) are as tactless, as stupid, and as apathetic about this as we look like being, it's just going to be George III and the Boston Tea Party and Co. all over again – with disastrous results all around.

We (you and I) have in this project a chance to make an exceedingly conspicuous and therefore potentially *useful* gesture in favour of Anglo-Canadian co-operation.

I have never before felt so convinced of the obvious practical value of anything I've been asked to be connected with. This is the more striking because we needn't be mixed up with the pompous frustrating machinery of Councils and Government Departments. We deal with Tom (whom I find to be most sensible and trustworthy, with the drive of a jet-engine and a wisdom beyond his years) and quite a small committee which is, as yet, humble and malleable.

I say "as yet" because it has not as yet tasted the heady wine of success. The real test of this whole business won't begin till the first fences have been successfully leaped, till the second and even third Festival.

Smaller aspects:

Repertoire – I should have thought two plays. That gives one a second barrel in case the first misfires. But three productions become a bit unwieldy and confuses the issue in a network of mechanics and small practical difficulties of casting and dressmaking and assistant stage-management. But there may be over-riding reasons for doing a third play.

I feel strongly that at all events in the first year, the repertoire should be entirely Shakespearean. You should, in my opinion, play *Hamlet* and then something in bold contrast. . . . But this choice is really your affair primarily.

Bear in mind that the audience will – unquestionably – be exceedingly unsophisticated. But one mustn't confuse unsophisticated with unintelligent.

Canadian Actors: the field must obviously be carefully explored. From what I've seen (and heard on the radio) there certainly is a good deal of talent. At this stage it would be daft to be dogmatic, but I think one should envisage the project *Something* like this: . . . .

	you
	I
*I suggest Moiseiwitsch	a designer*
**I suggest Cecil Clarke	stage manager**
	four or five actors
	two actresses

What a long, long letter. I do hope it's given you some of the sort of *impressions* you want; you can get all *information* from Tom.

I do most eagerly and keenly hope you'll embark on this project, dear Alec. Please show this letter to Tom so that he's kept in the picture in view of the need to get as far as we can.

(signed)
Tony

When I finally had a chance to read this letter after the meeting with Guinness, I was struck with awe. Here was a director who had been connected with the Old Vic, the Edinburgh Festival, Israel's Habimah Theatre, New York's Metropolitan Opera, and much more, and our non-existent, non-financed idea for a festival in Canada had the most "practical value" of anything he had been involved in.

I should have been terrified. What were we doing? Could we pull it off? But by this time, we were all so completely sure that, as Harry Showalter had said at Guthrie's first meeting with the committee, "We want to do something of significance," that the thought of failing never entered our heads.

In order to get "as far as we can" on the "project," I was soon off to obtain the services of those two, then-unknown-to-me theatre people, Moiseiwitsch and Clarke.

At one point during my hectic trip to England, sometime between when I obtained the services of Alec Guinness, lost the services of Alec Guinness, and gained them once more, I was reminded by Tony Guthrie, "You'll need a designer for this."

I nearly blurted out "What's a designer?" but decided to keep quiet.

"I don't want to force you on this, but as I told you back in Canada, I strongly suggest that you try and get Tanya Moiseiwitsch."

I hardly needed forcing. I figured if Tyrone Guthrie mentioned her, then she *must* be good. I did not know then that their two careers were very much entwined. In 1944, Tony had offered her the job of designer with the Old Vic's Liverpool Playhouse company, where she costumed *Dr. Faustus, The School for Scandal,* and more. The "poetic realism" shown in her later production of the Old Vic's *Uncle Vanya,* starring Sir Laurence Olivier, Sir Ralph Richardson, and Dame Sybil Thorndike, had placed her among Britain's top theatrical designers. Her designs for Shakespeare's history cycle at Stratford-on-Avon in 1951 had only enhanced her reputation.

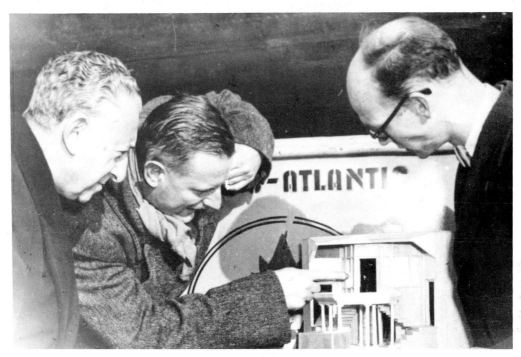

ABOVE Tyrone Guthrie shows the model of Tanya Moiseiwitsch's apron stage to his old friend Rupert Caplan of Montreal CBC and Tom Patterson at the Montreal airport.

RIGHT Tom Orr and his wife in the Shakespearean garden he planned and fought for in the early part of the century. (*Walter Curtain/Public Archives of Canada/PA-155897*)

BELOW The first budget, which Patterson made up some time in late 1951. (*Stratford Festival Archives*)

ABOVE The blessing of the sod-turning ceremony by board member Archdeacon Lightbourne. *From left to right*, contractor Oliver Gaffney, architect Bob Fairfield, Mayor Laurence Feick, three enthusiastic Stratfordians, Tom Patterson (behind the Archdeacon), board members Norm Kaye, Dr. John Penistan, Helen Griffith,and Bill Kalbfleisch, Festival supporter Dr. Joe Boyd, and board members Shirley Anderson and Alf Bell. (*The Beacon-Herald*)

LEFT The same scene staged for the NFB film *The Stratford Adventure*. *Left to right*, Tom Patterson, Harry Showalter, Marionne Johnston (a Stratfordian in the 1953 company), Fred Edwards, MPP, and Mayor Laurence Feick. (*The Beacon-Herald*)

BELOW Tom Patterson and Harry Showalter in 1953. (*Public Archives of Canada/C-49590*)

TOP A meeting such as this took place almost daily throughout the construction period. *Left to right*, Bob Fairfield, Cecil Clarke, Tanya Moiseiwitsch, Tyrone Guthrie, Alf Bell, and Tom Patterson. (*Stratford Festival Archives*)

ABOVE Contractor Oliver Gaffney and architect Bob Fairfield watch as the first sod is bulldozed. (*The Beacon-Herald*)

RIGHT Douglas Rain and Tyrone Guthrie manage to smile even amid the chaos of construction (*Courtesy of Arnie's Café*)

TOP LEFT Alec Guinness takes his first look at the "muddy hole." Production manager Cecil Clarke, despite his look of despair, carried on as if "All's Well." (*Peter Smith & Co.*)

CENTRE Eight or nine weeks before opening night, the two backstage poles were finally in position and the unique stage was almost finished. (*C. Lund/Public Archives of Canada/PA-111358*)

TOP RIGHT Before rehearsals began, the company threw a party for Stratfordians. Here Irene Worth, Alec Guinness, Judy and Tony Guthrie shake hands with local supporters. (*Stratford Festival Archives*)

ABOVE Jessica Tandy and Hume Cronyn were the first major theatrical donors to the Festival. (*Stratford Festival Archives*)

LEFT Tyrone Guthrie explains the stage to Hume Cronyn, who came from New York for the party, and to Beatrice Taylor, drama critic of the *London Free Press*. (*Peter Smith & Co.*)

The "Toscanini" of tent makers,
Skip Manley, who lived in and protected
"her" for the entire season.
(Courtesy of John Reed)

LEFT The crew who, under Skip Manley's direction, raised the massive canvas. The man in the centre has often been incorrectly identified as Skip Manley. (*Peter Smith & Co.*)

BELOW The first canvas going over the stage. (*Peter Smith & Co.*)

BOTTOM A scene, staged for the NFB's cameras, of Patterson watching while Tony Guthrie conducts a rehearsal and Tanya Moiseiwitsch takes notes. (*Walter Curtin/Public Archives of Canada/PA-129866*)

LEFT Alec Guinness rehearses his lines backstage. (*Walter Curtin/ Public Archives of Canada/PA-122727*)

ABOVE In the middle of the construction site, Amelia Hall talks with Guthrie, as Judy Guthrie cools off with a drink. (*Walter Curtin/Public Archives of Canada/PA-137091*)

BELOW LEFT Jacqueline Cundall, the Head of Properties, discusses her work with Tanya and Tony in the O'Cedar Mop factory. (*Peter Smith & Co.*)

TOP Finally, it is up – the largest tent of its kind in the world. (*Peter Smith & Co.*)

LEFT Musical director Louis Applebaum discusses the score for *Richard III* with Tony Guthrie (*Walter Curtin [NFB]/Public Archives of Canada/PA-122729*)

BELOW Alec Guinness welcomes his wife, Merula, and his son, Matthew, on their arrival in Stratford. (*NFB/Public Archives of Canada/PA-156506*)

Tony told me that Tanya was coming around to his London flat and invited me to join them. When I arrived, Tony, his wife, Judy, and the future designer of the Stratford, Ontario, Shakespearean stage were sitting around a radio, listening intently.

"I'd appreciate it if we did not start the meeting yet," Tony whispered to me, nodding at the audience of the concert in progress.

The beautiful music was being performed by Tanya's father, Benno Moiseiwitsch, the concert pianist, live from Albert Hall. (Years later, when the fine musician played with the Toronto Symphony, people kept approaching him and asking if he was any relation to Tanya, whose work they all knew from Stratford, Ontario!)

The radio concert was marvellous, and after the father had finished, the proud daughter turned to the Guthries and myself, and we got right down to business. Money was not an issue for her, as it had not been for Guinness, either. And also like Guinness, Tanya Moiseiwitsch was very eager to come. As she told a Stratford interviewer some thirty years after this meeting, "When Guthrie said, would I like to go to Canada, I couldn't believe my luck or couldn't believe my ears." She, along with Tony, had also been working away at breaking down the proscenium stage, and she saw the Stratford Festival as a glorious opportunity to work on the apron stage she and Tony had long desired.

Next came another crucial ingredient for our Festival stew: Cecil Clarke. Once again, Guthrie took me by the hand.

"I don't want to load you down with a bunch of Englishmen or anything like that, but I really think that you need a good production manager. You see, there hasn't been enough theatre in Canada to produce the kind of person who knows how to pull all of this together."

He continued his lesson: "Cecil Clarke is production manager of the Old Vic, and I think that he might be interested in coming," Tony said. "Why don't you go and see him?"

And so I visited the Old Vic, a place that I'd heard about for years, but had never seen. I found myself once again

walking into a major theatrical institution, talking to important men and women of the arts, and hiring them. And with
no money behind me to offer!

Cecil Clarke was quite small, even shorter than myself,
but quite dapper and very, very English. He was militaristic
but pleasant-looking; clean-shaven, and was never without
a tie. He radiated brilliance. I was not sure if he had spoken
with Guthrie, but I had been told by Tony that once I
mentioned Tanya's name, I would be welcome.

When I first met Clarke, I invited him to come over to
Canada and be our "stage manager." Yes, I had the terms
mixed up. (Indeed, I was so unknowledgeable about theatre,
I did not even know the difference between stage and
production managers!)

"Well, uh. . .er, really," stammered Cecil. "You know, at
the Old Vic, I'm a little bit higher than stage manager!" He
said this, thank heavens, with a very friendly smile on his
face.

"I'm sorry," I blushed. "I don't know these terms. What
exactly are you, here?"

"Production manager," he said.

"Yeah. That's what I mean. Would you be our production
manager?"

He agreed.

It was Guthrie's magic again, of course. And, once again,
money was never at issue. Cecil Clarke's attitude was, "Great.
I can work with Tony again on something new!"

Clarke was a brilliant man, and as it turned out, the
Stratford Festival could not have been put together without
him. Even before the Festival got fully under way, he worked
with Guthrie on the entire production system – wardrobe,
properties, the construction of the theatre itself – and even
assisted in fundraising. His past suggested what an asset
he would be: He was one of the three people who had made
the Old Vic such a success after the war. Indeed, when he
was only twenty-one, he had been in charge of the British
sector of Berlin, as a colonel. Clearly, he was much more
important than a stage manager!

S

My excitement steadily mounted during the trip to England. "Boy, *look!*" I would almost cry aloud, "We've lined up all these major theatre people! It's really going now!" But then, as I have noted before, I never doubted that it would come together; I had this boundless confidence.

During my stay, I constantly phoned and wrote to Stratford. And, as always, I was supported mightily by the newspapers of Canada, which picked up the stories from the wire. "LONDON (CP) – Alec Guinness, versatile star of stage and screen, and Tyrone Guthrie, former director of the Old Vic theatre, have agreed to visit Canada next summer for a proposed Shakespearean festival at Stratford, Ont., it was announced today. . . .Tanya Moiseiwitsch, scenery designer, has expressed definite interest in the proposed festival."

Even *La Presse* of Montreal reported that "Le remarquable acteur de la scène et de l'écran anglais Alec Guinness, et le metteur en scène Tyrone Guthrie, ancien directeur du Théatre du Old Vic, ont consenti à se render au Canada l'été prochain en vue du Festival shakespearien que l'on projette de donner à Stratford, en Ontario." On the same date (October 1, 1952), Herbert Whittaker had a major article under the headline "THREE TOP BRITISH THEATRE FOLK PLAN SHAKESPEARE FESTIVAL IN CANADA." But most remarkable of all, *The Times* of London, England, reported, under the heading SHAKESPEARIAN FESTIVAL FOR ONTARIO, "It was announced in London yesterday by Ontario House that Mr. Alec Guinness, Mr. Tyrone Guthrie, and Miss Tanya Moiseiwitsch, the stage designer, have agreed to take part in. . . ."

But glory and fame were not yet mine to claim, much less grasp. When my plane landed at the Malton airport, just west of Toronto, there was nobody to welcome me home. I had expected at least someone to greet me, but no such luck. I felt like an immigrant, and it was a terrible let-down. I had landed four aces of contemporary theatre – Guthrie, Guinness, Moiseiwitsch, and Clarke, but no one else had shown up to play the game.

7

The Hard Part Begins

"Mr. Patterson is back from his British trip with amazement and satisfaction in about equal parts, I'd say," wrote Herb Whittaker in the October 17, 1952 edition of *The Globe and Mail*. "His mission has been notably successful. I think his own devotion to the cause of a Stratford Festival must have been his greatest asset. . . ."

My devotion was far less important than the remarkable generosity of the wonderful people who had agreed to come to Stratford. The total amount of money promised to Guthrie, Guinness, and Moiseiwitsch was around $12,000 – less than Judy Garland had *turned down* for a single week's work the previous summer at Toronto's Melody Fair. The expenses, according to the minutes of the October 17, 1952, committee meeting, were $4,500 for Tony Guthrie, $5,500 for Alec Guinness, and $1,200 for Tanya Moiseiwitsch, plus expenses and fares for spouses and children. When Harry Showalter heard about this, he declared, "I just can't bring myself to believe that people are this way, but I'm having it proved in front of my eyes."

Out of eyesight, there was much happening on the other side of the ocean, as Guthrie wrote in his autogiography:

Guinness and I read all the plays of Shakespeare, met often and discussed, inconclusively, which we should suggest to the committee at Stratford.

Miss Moiseiwitsch and I, who are old collaborators, had long dreamed of such a stage as was now to come into being. We were agreed that, while conforming to the conventions of the Elizabethan theatre in practicalities, it should not present a pseudo-Elizabethan appearance. We were determined to eschew *Ye Olde*. Rough sketches on the backs of envelopes gave place to careful drawings. Like every good designer, Moiseiwitsch knows not only what she wants a thing to look like, but why; and she also knows how it is made. Drawings gave place to detailed construction plans. Finally a model was made – an exact replica of the stage which was eventually built – to the scale of a half-inch representing one foot.

By the end of 1952, Guinness and I had narrowed down the choice of play. We felt that in one of the two plays he must play a star part; in the other his part should not dominate, the emphasis should be on the team. We felt, moreover, that the two plays should contrast, that it would be a mistake to suggest two histories, two comedies, or two tragedies.

Richard III was agreed upon fairly soon. Guinness wanted to play it; I agreed that it was a suitable vehicle. We both felt that the complicated genealogy, the rather obscure historical background, were probably drawbacks for Canadian audiences but might be offset by the strong thread of melodrama.

For the second play we suggested *All's Well*, largely because it offers such an even distribution of good parts, and because of the bold contrast to *Richard III*. Its unfamiliarity, which would be a handicap to popularity in London, seemed to matter less in Stratford where all the Shakespearean plays were almost equally unfamiliar. We also felt that it would make for a better team-feeling between the British and Canadian actors, if one of the two plays were as new to us as to them.

The plays I was plugging with the Stratford committee were *Hamlet* and *Julius Caesar*, but whether those were the plays chosen was the least of my concerns. First, I had to report to Maclean-Hunter as my leave of absence had been only for six weeks. I met with Floyd Chalmers, and as always, he was marvellous.

"Look, Tom," he said. "This thing is too big for Canada, that we should stand in your way. Now, what do you want to do? Do you wish to stay as you have been, with *Civic Administration* magazine, and go up to Stratford on weekends; do you want to work part-time, or do you want to quit now? You have to make up your own mind, and we'll go along with it."

"Really," I declared, "I think that I'd better quit."

"That's fine," said Chalmers.

On October 18, 1952, *The Beacon-Herald* blared, "FESTIVAL PROJECT IS APPROVED/TOM PATTERSON TO BE MANAGER." It was a given that I would be manager; no one ran against me. Remember, the other people on the committee had real jobs in the outside world. It was good that the Stratford Shakespearean Festival of Canada was incorporated at about the same time – but we still had no money!

So I found myself working full-time on the Festival, although we had no office. I told the committee, "We are going to have to set up an office, and we must have a letterhead, and we should have a typewriter and a typist."

In those days, in our city, all this could be obtained for around $3,500. It was hardly Hollywood First Class, but it was a beginning.

This led to a new crisis – one among many. The bank manager who had organized the loan of the money to send me to England had been moved while I was overseas, and a new bank manager had been appointed. The committee thought, understandably, that they would merely go back and double their loan.

The new bank manager replied to their request: "No way! This crazy, bloody scheme – what are you talking about?" The people who were willing to sign for the loan were the leading doctors and lawyers of Stratford, but he still refused to accept their signatures.

It was now approaching Christmas – barely seven months

before the first performance of the new Stratford Festival –
and there were the usual Christmas parties, for which my
native town is famous.

At one party, which I went to with my wife, another
Stratford bank manager showed up. He started talking to
my wife and got her into a corner.

"Hey! This idea of Tom's. Boy, it's great! How can I get
in on it?"

My wife said, "I think there is a pretty easy way."

She soon reported this conversation to me, and I quickly
started to talk to him. The next day, I approached several
committee members and stated, "He wants in on it. Why
don't we try and spring a loan from him?"

Which we did. This is how the Royal Bank lost the Stratford
Festival account, and the Bank of Montreal won it. In the
meantime – and mean times they were – I was existing on
personal loans from my own bank manager. I worked for
three full months for no pay. (Others who would be involved
in the Festival, namely our big-name star, were doing a lot
better. A film called *The Lavender Hill Mob*, starring Stanley
Holloway and Alec Guinness, opened at Stratford's Avon
Theatre shortly after Christmas, 1952. Despite its popularity,
it caused some to cast aspersions on the Festival. In his
column, *Showplace*, Toronto Star writer Jack Karr wrote, in
late January 1953, "When the Stratford (Ont.) Shakespearean
Festival is staged next July, airlines will be running special
flights daily from New York to bring the Broadway crowd
up. But would they bother coming at all if Alec Guinness
weren't to be starred?")

During the fall, the committee decided to regroup as
another body, independent of the Chamber of Commerce.
This took place at one of those fantastic legal meetings, which
I have never understood. It seemed that we had over a dozen
meetings within fifteen minutes, where one committee dis-
banded, a second committee was formed, the thing was
passed over to a third committee, and then to a fourth, and
so on. And these were all the same people!

At that fateful meeting on November 1, 1952, we ended
up as the Board of Directors of the Stratford Shakespearean
Festival Foundation of Canada. (A few years later, they

changed their name, once more, to "the Board of Governors," because too many of them were being asked "How can *you* be the director? Tyrone Guthrie is!")

The Stratford Shakespearean Festival Foundation was incorporated with a Canadian federal charter. The board comprised all the previous committee's members. It was a non-profit corporation, which meant that contributions would be tax-deductible. And boy, did we need them. There was no Canada Council, no Ontario Arts Council we could turn to for grants; these councils would not come into existence for several more years.

The government grants we received for our inaugural season totalled a whopping $5,500. Five thousand dollars came from the City of Stratford. The other $500 came after a rather charming runaround. It was in early 1953, when the money crunch was at its worst. I met with Leslie Frost, the premier of Ontario, and requested financial assistance.

"The only way I see that we can give you money is through the Department of Education," he told me. He then phoned the minister of that department, Dr. Dunlop, and made an appointment for me.

When I met with Dr. Dunlop, he told me, "We have no money for theatre. The only way we can do anything is if you can show that this Stratford Festival is educational."

So I returned to Stratford and made up a letter which proved, beyond a shadow of a doubt, that Shakespeare was educational. And we got our $500 grant.

Interestingly, the first *real* impetus we had in fundraising came from the world of J. Arthur Rank. Very early on, Leonard Brockington, the titular head of Rank of Canada, a cultured, articulate man, and the first president of the CBC, promised that Rank would donate $15,000 to the Festival. Soon after, John Davis, the international head of the firm, flew out from England, and he changed the promise slightly: "We will give the *last* fifteen thousand." (I think that, along with many others, he believed that the Festival would never take place, and I do not blame him for that.) Rank did live up to its original promise, although its grant came so late – shortly before we opened, when the tent was already up and the performers were all here – that they got no publicity whatsoever! But I cannot overestimate the importance of that initial offer of $15,000, which I had taken back to the board with such excitement!

On his own initiative, Tyrone Guthrie had already talked to many expatriate Canadian actors, who had gone to England because of the lack of opportunity in Canadian theatre. But in early December 1952, Tony returned to Canada for what he described as "interviews" (as opposed to "auditions"). Pat Pearce wrote about the visit in *The Montreal Herald*, on December 5: "It was old home week for Mr. Guthrie, who spent six months in Montreal, twenty years ago, associated with Rupert Caplan, on a series of radio plays for the CNR ["we were a kind of annex of the parcels department," Tony had written of his work back then], followed by a cross-country trip which made him many life-long friends and began a continued interest in Canadian affairs."

Over five days, in Montreal, Ottawa, and Toronto, Guthrie saw a total of 317 people, narrowing them down to about sixty "probables." Letters were then sent to these men and women saying that we would be grateful if they would tell us before they made any other definite commitments between May and August 1953. So great was the interest in the theatrical community that a mere three of the five dozen approached turned down the eventual offer. Lloyd Bochner, later one of North America's major television stars, paid his own fare from New York to Toronto for an interview. Many others would have done the same, but decided to wait when they heard that Guthrie would be visiting Manhattan, after his trip to Canada.

Tony did not believe in auditions. As he once told me, "People who give good auditions are never really any good on stage, and good actors can rarely give a good audition." I was disappointed at first, as I wanted to watch these actors perform, albeit briefly. Most interviews lasted only three or four minutes; none was longer than ten minutes. These men and women were expecting quite a challenge, and they would come in all tensed up. Guthrie would ask, "What is your name?"

"You've got it *there!*" some would say, pointing to the sheet he had in front of him.

"True," he would answer. "But I just wanted to talk with you. What are your ideas? I mean, why would you like to be in the company?"

The prospective Festival performer would reply, and Tony would scribble some notes next to his or her name. A highlight was when one woman came in one morning at about ten o'clock, all made up like a Hollywood starlet. Tony wrote down, "Would make a good tart." (She was not chosen for the Stratford company; Guthrie felt that all her make-up and fancy dress were not appropriate for a pre-lunch interview.)

He met with the artists in a hotel in Montreal, at the Canadian Repertory Theatre in Ottawa, and at the New Play Society offices in Toronto. I was with him all the time. Once we took a train together from Montreal to the capital, and we sat directly across from Mike Pearson, the future Nobel Peace Prize winner and Prime Minister of Canada. He was then in External Affairs, and he spent the whole journey ploughing through papers on his lap. I whispered to Tony, "That's Mike Pearson," and was pleasantly surprised to hear that he knew immediately who Pearson was.

On this visit to Canada, Tony Guthrie had brought Tanya's model of the stage with him. The first time I saw it was on the tarmac of the Dorval Airport near Montreal. Rupert Caplan, the well-known CBC producer who had worked with Guthrie nearly a quarter-century earlier on a radio series about the CNR, was there to greet him. There was also a photographer present. Tony opened a large box and displayed the stunning stage. I had thought it was marvellous that this woman, Tanya Moiseiwitsch, had created such an impressive model – although I had no idea whatsoever just how revolutionary it was. And to do so much work for no pay!

In retrospect, one of the exceptional factors about the Stratford theatre is that the first thing that was designed was the stage. We were not constructing a building, we were constructing a theatre, underlining the point that where the actors perform – the stage – is most important of all.

We were also building public interest, and, we hoped, public financial support. Tony displayed the stage in each city he visited in early December, describing it proudly as "the only one of its kind in the world today." He gave public lectures in each community. Trans-Canada Air Lines (later Air Canada), offered to fly four planes a day from New York to London, Ontario, with special buses from London to Stratford, for the Festival.

"GUTHRIE SEES STRATFORD FESTIVAL IMPORTANT TO CANADIAN THEATRE" read the headline in dozens of newspapers across the country, compliments of Canadian Press, when the director arrived in Montreal. "SHAKESPEARE FESTIVAL STILL A GAMBLE, ASSERTS GUTHRIE" read a story out of Toronto on December 11, after Guthrie spoke at the Museum Theatre of the Royal Ontario Museum.

But if the Stratford Festival was really to be "important to Canadian theatre," and not be merely "a gamble," then we had to do something around Tanya Moiseiwitsch's inspired design. We had to find an architect who could plan a building around that beautiful stage. Guthrie had previously written to me and requested that I line up a number of them for him to talk to when he arrived in Canada.

I dug up the names of all the leading architects in Toronto at that time and set up appointments with each. The plan was not just to go and see them; rather we had decided to invite them in groups to Tony's hotel room, where the model of the stage would be set up for them to examine.

Each group came in, and Guthrie gave each a lecture. To this day, I regret that we did not have a tape recorder set up, because he spoke articulately, and at great length, about his philosophy of the apron stage. Not one architect had the slightest idea of what he was talking about.

It must be remembered that very few in Canada even knew who Tyrone Guthrie was. At these meetings, he was treated by the architects like some artsy-craftsy guy who had the nerve to come in and tell *them* how to build a theatre. One architect actually told Guthrie, "Look. You don't have to go through all that, because we just finished designing the Odeon Hyland cinema, up on St. Clair Avenue." I thought that Tony was going to hit the roof.

Another architect, who appeared to have at least a smidgen of understanding of what Guthrie was talking about, was told, "Take the model. Go and study it for a couple of days, and we'll meet again."

The man returned for a second meeting with Guthrie and myself. The architect looked at the stage one more time, and then queried, "There's one thing that bothers me: Where do the footlights go?"

So much for insight! The entire principle of the apron stage – that you lose the separation of the audience from the performer – was completely missed by the man.

Sometime later, Tony Guthrie said to me, "Tom, there's an old friend in Toronto whom I worked with years ago, on that CNR radio drama. I know that he's in this city, and I realize that you're paying me, so I shouldn't be doing things on my own. But if I was in Toronto and failed to call him and at least say 'hello,' it would be just terrible."

I agreed, of course, never suspecting that in that old acquaintanceship would lie the answer to the problem of the theatre. I called the man – Dr. Ned Corbett – and arranged for him to meet us for a drink at the University Club. While the British director and his Canadian chum were talking about old times and their families, Corbett mentioned that his daughter had just married a young architect.

Guthrie and I both looked at each other, wondering whether we should ask to meet his son-in-law, or whether this would create another embarrassing situation. Eventually, Tony asked if we could get together with the fellow. A lunch was quickly arranged with Ned Corbett's daughter's husband, whose name was Bob Fairfield.

When we met, the three of us talked about the weather in Canada, and the weather in England, and about the extraordinary difference between the weather in England and the weather here. In other words, we were afraid to bring up the real purpose of the meeting.

Finally, Bob Fairfield blurted out, "Hey, I don't know what you've got me here for, because I don't know the first damned thing about building theatres."

Guthrie pointed his finger at the young architect and exclaimed, "You're hired!"

And so Fairfield became our architect. We gave him the model of the stage, with its balcony and its trap-door, and invited him to invent the best way to cover it. By that time, we had already pretty well decided to use a tent.

We had no time to dither around; this was early December, and we were to open the following July. Right from the beginning, we knew that he had to design the tent over that stage, the bowl/amphitheatre, and everything else. The bowl is still there, over a third-of-a-century later, and it is the same one that we opened with, back in 1953. The only major difference between the theatre today and the 1953 version is that, in the tent, we were unable to have balcony seating.

That first season, the seats in the end sections did not give a very good view of the stage. So when we finally built the permanent building, we cut off the end sections, and a bit more, to improve the circle. The seats we removed from the circle were added to the new balcony.

One of the first problems we encountered was the status of the rock on which our Peter would build our Church: Who owned the land? Obviously, the theatre had to be designed for a certain site. The land we had chosen, we found, was roughly three-quarters owned by the Stratford Board of Parks, and one-quarter owned by the Ontario government.

A survey had to be completed, from which we found out that there were no records, and nobody knew exactly where the boundary line between the two properties lay. But it was all the same parkland, no matter who owned it. We realized that we would have to deal with both the Parks Board and the Ontario government. The latter gave us permission to use the land for the summer, providing that we put it back to the same condition in which we found it. Fat chance!

When we eventually built the permanent theatre and removed the end seats, it was necessary to cut into the reinforced concrete. The Foundation Company of Canada was unable to get saws strong enough to cut the thick concrete.

That's how temporary a structure it was; may the Ontario government and the Good Lord forgive us.

The craziness of this agreement with the Powers That Were regarding the land was underlined in the second year of the Festival. And although it is terribly unchronological, this is the place to tell that strange tale.

During the first year of the Festival, four massive tent poles kept the tent aloft; two backstage and two in the auditorium. Unfortunately, the two in the auditorium blocked the sight-lines of a number of theatre-goers. So, in the second year of the Festival, we took these poles out and obtained even bigger ones, which we placed outside, hanging the front of the tent from them. But one of those poles was, alas, on the provincial government land, and the other was on – you guessed – the Parks Board land.

By this time, the Festival was a huge success, so we went with some confidence to the provincial government's deputy minister, who declared, "We might as well not waste any time on this, because you are going to get it anyway. So go ahead." Time was, of course, of the essence, because if the issue had not been settled quickly, the theatre would not have been completed on time, and the show could not have gone on.

The Parks Board was to meet the following week. So I approached the tent-master, Skip Manley – one of the heroes of this book; more on him later – and told him, "We've got permission to put up the tent-pole on the left-hand side, and we get permission for the right-hand side next week."

"Oh, yeah; the left-hand side," Manley stated.

Oops. I was facing Skip when I told him which side, and he was referring to *his* left, not mine, when he replied to my directions.

So Skip Manley, tent-maker extraordinaire, but more gauche than droit, put up the giant tent-pole on the Parks Board land first, before permission had been obtained.

The following week, the Parks Board had its meeting, and the item regarding its land came up. Since they were all Stratford people, they decided to go down to the theatre and see for themselves where this pole was going to go.

They visited the location, and there it was: the world's biggest tent-pole, sunk deep into their land.

The front portion of the theatre, including most, if not all of the auditorium, was on Ontario government land. Land that was to be returned in the condition in which it was found. But from the very beginning, all of us knew damned well that it wasn't going to be. If we had kept our promise, the Stratford Festival would have been in ruins.

"Well, I guess there's not much we can do about this," the Parks people said.

And that was that.

Oh, yes – the building permit? It arrived two full weeks *after* the Stratford Festival opened, in late July 1953.

8

For love, not money

STRATFORD SHAKESPEAREAN FESTIVAL FOUNDATION

CAMPAIGN FOR FUNDS

(1) It will advertise the city, as it has already done, over the whole North American continent as well as in England;

(2) With a conservative estimate of 30,000 people coming into the city, it will mean an extra income of at least $150,000 to our merchants and citizens;

(3) As well as ourselves, it will give our children and our children's children, an opportunity to see some of the best theatre in the world;

(4) It will completely reverse the usual trend in Stratford's summer. Instead of everybody leaving the city, everybody will be coming in.

HERE'S WHAT WE ARE ASKING OF STRATFORD'S CITIZENS:

(1) To contribute towards this project, so that every citizen can feel a part of it;

(2) To advertise it by word of mouth and by letter.

YOUR CONTRIBUTION WILL PAY LARGER DIVIDENDS AS WELL AS BEING AN INVESTMENT IN YOUR COMMUNITY AND NATION

I n February 1953, this quarter-page advertisement appeared in the Stratford *Beacon-Herald*. Donations, "large or small," were to be sent to W.H. Kalbfleisch, Treasurer, at the Bank of Montreal in Stratford. And, the advertisement screamed at the bottom: DONATIONS ARE INCOME TAX EXEMPT.

The board and myself, however, were hardly exempt from fears, concerns, and potential disasters. At the beginning, as I have noted, there was no money whatsoever. Tanya Moiseiwitsch received nothing for her model of the stage; I received nothing for my frequent speeches and non-stop rabble-rousing. Indeed, in the early stages there were no contracts. (Alec Guinness's arrived from his agents in England well into the playing period, but this did not stop him from working.) We all just dug in and did everything we could. Phrases such as "That's not my job" were not to be heard within fifty miles of Stratford, Ontario.

I have always assumed that we opened our office in late 1952, and so I was stunned to discover in 1986 that we did not move into our Festival headquarters until mid-March, barely four months before opening night. It was not until February 23, 1953, that we placed this advertisement in *The Beacon-Herald*: "Stenographer-Secretary required. Must have knowledge of shorthand with some office experience. Excellent working conditions." (That last line is no example of Truth in Advertising.)

A few weeks before, I had asked Florence Pelton, a switchboard operator at the Whyte Packing Company and my future sister-in-law, if she would be interested in helping out. In her straightforward way, she said, "I'll think about it." After the advertisement appeared, she *did* think about it and phoned my mother to ask, "Do you think Tom is still interested in having me?" We hired her with no assurance that this would be a permanent job, but she ended up working for the Festival for over twenty-five years.

Soon after this, we also hired Fran Tomkins as part-time (later full-time) secretary/typist. Fran, who was tall, thin, and prematurely white-haired, quickly became, and remained for many years, a major face and force on the Stratford Festival.

We rented, for practically nothing, some space above a bank at the corner of Downie and Market Square in downtown Stratford. Now, 139 Downie Street, which was the correct address of our office, did not sound very impressive to me. Equally unimpressive was the office's entrance. To get to it, we had to enter through the back door and climb up some rather gloomy stairs. So, when we were designing our letterhead, I hesitated over our uninspiring address.

Then I thought, "If we're going to be a country festival, let's be *really* country." So I created our own, special address: One Market Place. I was told later that when our letters arrived at such big-city institutions as *The New York Times*, the critics were charmed by it. And, although there was no such address, our local post office accepted it happily. But then, such were the ways of most of the people of Stratford.

Our Toronto office, which was donated by Jimmy Cowan, one of Canada's greatest publicists, and stockbroker John Frame (both members of the Stratford Old Boys' Committee, although the former was actually from the town of Shakespeare, a half-dozen miles down the road), was opened in October or November 1952. Through Jimmy, we acquired the services of Mary Joliffe, who had been a school teacher in China and in rural Ontario before becoming our publicist.

The office was sparsely furnished, but it was out of these two rooms, in a building on the corner of Dundas and Victoria Streets in downtown Toronto, that Mary Joliffe – with Cowan's help – set up the publicity operation which was to become a model for theatrical companies right across the North American continent.

By this time, things were already getting pretty hectic, what with Guthrie's visits, the auditions/interviews taking place, and all the gossip and conjecture about what was going on. In spite of all this interest, there was still very little, if any, money.

As a result, when a press release had to go out, we would scrounge among ourselves to raise the money to purchase another package of mimeograph paper from the nearby Grand & Toy stationery store.

Finally, work began to pile up, and we realized that we simply had to have some secretarial assistance. And so, with the help of that Old Boys' Committee, we hired a young woman by the name of Vera Mackenzie. It seemed to take her less than half an hour to size up the situation. And having come from well-financed offices, she started to organize us – a pretty difficult job, because neither Mary nor I were particularly "organizable" in standard office procedures. And that is being generous to us, too.

Since all the offices that Vera had worked in before had been very well supplied, she thought the idea of our buying mimeograph paper box by box from retail stores was "ridiculous." So through some former contact, she went ahead and ordered the blank paper wholesale.

It seemed like a good idea at the time. But when the paper all arrived, the delivery men wondered if our office was large enough to store it. With typical efficiency – and bravado – Vera told them, "Sure! Bring it in here!" indicating her office.

So they stacked the reams from floor to ceiling, completely covering all four walls, like men in the trenches of the Great War piling up sandbags. It seemed enough paper to last many years. But when we remonstrated her, Vera replied, "It's a lot cheaper this way, and you're going to use it all, anyway. You'll see."

What could we answer?

The next day, the board was arriving to inspect our Toronto office. When they saw all the paper stacked up and down each wall, there was real consternation.

"What are these people *doing* down here?" they asked. But the deed was done, and there was no way to return it.

And Vera was right, after all. The way the Stratford Festival snowballed, the mountains of paper were gone before Alec Guinness first put on his make-up to play Richard III.

By early 1953, our offices were organized, and our Festival board was working remarkably well together. From the first moment that Tanya's model was displayed on the Dorval runway until the theatre was built, there were regular meetings between the building committee, headed by Hans Buscher; the architect, Bob Fairfield; the contractor, Oliver Gaffney; the contractor's superintendent; Cecil Clarke; and, when they were in town, Tanya and Tony as well. (Tanya did not come to Stratford until February or March; Tony did not return until May.) They would gather at the drop of a hat, so that if a problem arose, it would be solved then and there.

We now had to attend to the serious business of money. There had been no professional theatre of any account before in Canada, and no new major theatre had been built in North America for a half-century. Indeed, these were the years of the coming of television, and theatres were closing up right across the continent. To go out and ask for money for a theatre seemed to be a pretty rash thing to do. We decided to raise as much as we could from local sources before we formally approached the rest of the Canadian public.

My very first projected budget for the Stratford, Ontario, Shakespearean Festival, scrawled in my little notebook sometime in the fall of 1952, was rather modest, to say the least. It read Stars $25,000, Cast $13,000, Tent, etc. $30,000, Admin. $20,000, Publicity $10,000, Costumes $3,000, Tickets, Staff, etc. $2,000, and so on, for a grand, not to mention a very unrealistic total of $117,000. In other words, approximately what they spend on coffee and snacks on the set of the average movie in the mid-1980s.

The board now had a charter and we were all working hard on a day-to-day basis. But in February 1953, we were in crisis. Either we had to raise some funds, or we had to fold.

There were many clues of this growing crisis. A letter from an architectural firm in Toronto to Tyrone Guthrie in London, dated January 6, 1953, included the lines: "We understood that the preliminary budget was set at $35,000. . . . When we met you in Toronto and saw the model of the stage, I could see that $35,000 was a nonsensical figure." To which Tony Guthrie wrote back, a few weeks later, in a masterpiece of British drollery,

As I think you know, the budgetary side of the Festival

has nothing to do with me. I cannot, therefore, discuss whether that had anything to do with the breaking off of negotiations between the Committee and your firm. I should imagine not. I think I shall be quite open with you and I hope you'll think this is a more friendly course than the easier one of being politely evasive. I did report to the Festival Committee that I was not greatly impressed with the amount of "prep" that had been done by you and your colleagues in connection with this particular assignment.

This impression was based on questions about the lighting, and a question about where the curtain was to fall, which, I must honestly admit, shook me somewhat. They suggested – and I made it *very* clear to the Committee that I might well be mistaken – that the elements of the problem had still to be grasped.

Less than six months before the "curtain was to go up" on the Festival, a prospective builder had yet to figure out that Guthrie's stage was to have no curtain! But our biggest worry was our budget, which was utterly unconnected to reality.

The board decided that we had to get the first money from the people of Stratford, Ontario. It was clear that we could not expect to obtain any money from the outside unless Stratford folk proved that they were interested.

In early February 1953, our working budget was revised to $150,000. We figured that if Stratford put up $30,000 of that amount, this would prove the city's interest. Then, the rest of the money would pour in from all over Canada. We were full of enthusiasm, spouting such phrases as "How could anybody turn us down for a project like this?"

So we made the decision to go ahead with the campaign. In the meantime, of course, I had been on the radio frequently promoting the Festival, and the newspapers across Canada were continuing to plug it with as much passion as any author pushes his or her new book. As well, all 18,000 citizens of Stratford, Ontario, were talking it up daily, even hourly.

One of my favourite "news reports" was in the local paper, shortly before Christmas, 1952. "The Ladies' Aid of Ontario Street Baptist Church held a short business meeting Thursday afternoon at the church. Group leader Mrs. Fred Pearce opened the meeting with prayer and the singing of a Christmas carol. . . . Mrs. B. McKenzie gave Luke 2 as scripture reading. The speaker, Mrs. H. Flett, chose as her topic, "The Shakespearean Festival," which proved interesting and enjoyable. The singing of another carol and the Mizpah benediction closed the meeting."

It was gatherings such as this one, multiplied by hundreds across our town, which would make the Stratford Festival a success. Obviously we had God on our side.

A far more important public meeting took place at the Stratford YMCA in early February 1953. It had been called by the directors of the Stratford Shakespearean Festival of Canada Foundation to acquaint the public with the many steps that had been taken to that date, toward an opening barely five months later.

Most of the "heavies" were there: Harry Showalter; Cecil Clarke, who had arrived in January and was hard at work setting up the production department; Alf Bell of the finance committee, who filled everyone in on the history of the project to that date; and yours truly.

It was at this seminal meeting that "district people" – to quote *The Beacon-Herald* of February 6 – were asked to provide $30,000, and "donations of any size, from fifty cents to $5,000 or more, will be welcomed." All tax deductible, of course. Alf Bell calculated that it would cost $150,000 to build the stage and the tent to go over it, to make costumes, to pay salaries, and cover advertising costs.

If every seat at every performance sold, he calculated, at an average of three dollars each, this would bring in $145,000, leaving us with a shortfall of only $5,000 to be raised elsewhere. But because we had high hopes of making this Festival into a continuing project, not merely a one-summer wonder, we still had to raise the full $150,000. We all had hopes that within three to five years, the Festival would find itself with money in the bank. Even more important than the raising of money locally, however, was the symbolic meaning behind it. For the townspeople of Stratford and

environs to raise $30,000 among themselves would be con-
crete evidence to the rest of Canada that this Festival was
a genuine cultural effort, backed by the community, and not
merely a crying out for public funds by an uninterested,
laissez-faire bunch of people.

Cecil Clarke took the opportunity of this meeting at the
YMCA to give a lesson to those present on the Importance
of Culture. ("Canada, as you know, is progressing in every
way. Enormous industries are opening up everywhere.
Money is plentiful. But you cannot progress without a firm
background of the arts.") And, Harry Showalter noted, "even
on a commercial plane," the Shakespearean Festival would
be helpful to our city.

The newspaper reported Showalter's plea for support this
way: "Retailers would sell more goods; householders would
receive money for rooms rented; there would be employees
of the project itself. More important, it would be of value
to young people, if only in helping them to develop the right
use of the English language." (Surely, there is nothing funnier
than inadvertent humour, wouldst thou not agree?)

The problem was, as we were quickly made aware, that
to get $30,000 out of the citizens of Stratford, Ontario, was
"absolutely impossible," to quote many of our supporters
at the time. The most successful campaign in the city's history
up to that time had been for the Red Cross, for which $18,000
had been raised. If the Red Cross could get only $18,000 –
during the war, moreover – then how on earth could we hope
to raise $30,000 for a playwright who had been dead for
350 years, and who was not even a Canadian?

But we went ahead and opened the local campaign on
a Monday. By the following day we were so close to our
objective that we had to hold back the announcement of
some of the donations, as we knew that there were more
to come. On the Wednesday, we increased the objective to
$35,000 and by the following Tuesday, we had raised $42,000
from the people of Stratford alone.

We were surprised and delighted. The largest single contribution had been $5,000, and a few were in the $3,000 range.
The rest came in relatively small amounts.

Our response was understandable: "There's no problem!

We've overshot our goals!" Less than twenty thousand souls had provided us with an average of over two dollars from each man, woman, and child in the town. We had overshot our goal with no contributions from the outside – no government support – nothing.

We now felt that we were armed with the backing of the Stratford community and could conquer the rest of the country with ease. But this confidence was a chimera. It would take us three full months to raise another $5,000 from the other cities and provinces of Canada. Not that general interest had subisided; it was simply that the rest of Canada was unwilling to put its money where its sympathies were. In his February 25, 1953 column in *The Globe and Mail*, Herbert Whittaker related that "the Stratford Festival is arousing a remarkable response, with letters pouring in from Greenland's icy mountains to Oklahoma's strand. Literally. A Mr. Hilmar Sallee, for instance, writes from Thule, in Greenland, near the North Pole, full of admiration for Tyrone Guthrie, asking for reservations. . . . From Oklahoma somebody writes for tickets after hearing the Festival mentioned on Don McNeill's 'Breakfast Club' broadcast."

Great. But our elation was short-lived: Where was the *financial* support? We were now in a real crisis. By this time, we had commitments with Guthrie, Guinness, Moiseiwitsch, and Cecil Clarke, and were making further commitments to sixty-four Canadian actors and actresses. The theatre was already under construction; we had totally spent the $40,000 raised; and we owed something in the range of $37,000 to the contractor, Oliver Gaffney.

The banker of Gaffney Construction Company kept going after Oliver, telling him that to continue working was stupid. "Pull out now and cut your losses," he was urged. Because he knew we had a terrible time problem, instead of pulling out, Oliver Gaffney kept pulling his workers off other jobs, putting lights up, and working his crew literally twenty-four hours a day. And all without pay – without even a prayer of getting paid at that time. Many thought that he was out of his mind.

(After a later crisis meeting in May, when it was finally and definitely decided that we *would* forge ahead, I went to tell Oliver the good news. He exclaimed, "I knew that I had to go ahead, anyway. If I had stopped, it was obvious that the whole bubble would burst.")

Such was the kind of commitment shown by those who were supportive of the Festival. Nothing would stop them; absolutely nothing. Indeed, the fact there was nothing in the bank account did not stop them, either. Thank heavens for that reading of Luke 2, back in December. (Which begins, "And it came to pass in those days, that there went out a decree. . .that all the world should be taxed. . . . And all went to be taxed, every one into his own city.")

The only thing to do was to go back to the people of Stratford on another campaign.

9

The Crises Continue

Despite the financial crisis, the board decided, as Oliver Gaffney had done, to carry on regardless. There was still much work to be done.

In late February 1953, I received a lengthy letter from Guthrie, in which he put a number of concerns on paper. First of all, he wanted to hire Irene Worth to act the roles of Queen Margaret in *Richard III* and Helena in *All's Well*.

This American-born actress had received her theatrical training in Britain and had long been admired for "the musicality of her voice and her commanding presence," as one critic put it. After a brief stint on Broadway, she had made her London debut in 1946 in *The Time of Your Life*. She had performed in Eliot's *The Cocktail Party* at the Edinburgh Festival, and had played Desdemona in *Othello*, Helena in *A Midsummer Night's Dream*, and Lady Macbeth in *Macbeth* at the Old Vic. Tony's concern was that, as of February 24, the terms her agent was asking were "too high." Shortly after this letter, I received a cable from Tony, which expressed his belief that Irene Worth would yet be "reasonable." In the meantime he had contacted Guinness to discuss the possibility of Jessica Tandy, but she and Hume Cronyn were both soon "out," as they were committed until the end of May. (Both Tandy and the Canadian-born Cronyn were wonderful supporters of the Festival, both before and after the casting.)

Guthrie was upset that we had not yet secured contracts with Douglas Campbell and Michael Bates, the only other non-Canadian performers we were hiring, in addition to Guinness and Worth. Both the director and Cecil Clarke agreed that "there are no available actors of the ability and type to play two of the parts in *Richard III* in Canada." (Campbell would play Lord Hastings in *Richard III* and Parolles in *All's Well*; Bates, the Mayor of London and Lafeu, respectively.)

Both Clarke and Tanya Moiseiwitsch were determined to find a costume cutter whose work they knew, so they could be "more confident in the standard of workmanship on the dresses for *Richard III*." Tony suggested Ray Diffen, whose work they "both know and respect highly," as someone who would probably be available, once he completed work at the British Stratford. (Tanya had phoned Diffen and had asked him if he wished to come to Stratford, Canada. "Stratford where?" he asked. This response has become a byword in Wardrobes in England, New York, and Canada. One of his assistants, Pat Scott, when she heard the offer, declared "I want to go, too!" To this request, Ray replied, "You haven't got enough experience yet." The young woman finally did make it in 1958 and became head of the Stratford Wardrobe. She is now my wife.)

Diffen's visit to us was his first to this side of the Atlantic, and he went on from our Festival to work in New York. Guthrie asked me to confirm his participation by cable, if Cecil could make him an offer, so that it would become official. He would cost quite a bit more than the minimum, I was told, but "we all know from experience that a first-class cutter can save endless money by saving time." I followed through on the matter at once. (At the time, I did not even know what a cutter was, but I have since learned through my marriage to Pat, now the head of the National Ballet Wardrobe, how valuable Guthrie's advice was.)

Tony expressed his hope, echoing Cecil, that "we shall get splendid service in Canada when we want a standard article on the commercial market," but warned that we would run into "great difficulty, delay and expense where we need stuff that is not commercially available," such as military and special boots (for *All's Well*), wigs, armour and swords, theatrical make-up, and other material for costumes. The director also suggested that, were it not for import restrictions, much of the stuff could come from England. I recommended to Tony that those pieces which had to be ordered from Britain should be ordered immediately, and that the duties would probably not be prohibitive. I also considered going to Ottawa to see if those duties could be waived.

Both Tony and Guinness expressed concern about being required to do publicity work, once rehearsals had begun. To quote him directly: "I have consulted Guinness, and he requests the Committee to appreciate that he will not be available for any public or promotional activities *whatsoever* during the period of rehearsal. This must also apply to all the other artists. The productions must be as good as we can make them, and this involves absolute concentration upon the work of preparation. We will lay aside a period for photographs of each play in costume at a time determined by you, otherwise there can be no interruptions whatever for photographs, journalistic interviews and that sort of stuff.

"If I may venture to suggest – a Press conference with Guinness and leading actors should be held at the very beginning of rehearsals, followed by, on the same day, a biggish social 'Do' which would enable Stratford Society to shake us all by the hand. Then into purdah till opening. This is important and I want the Chairman's assurance that it will be so."

I informed Tony that I had turned down all requests for public appearances during the rehearsal period, and even suggested to Harry Showalter that he send a letter assuring him the same, as Tony felt so strongly about it. Yet, in spite of these rather strong demands, and our acceptance of them, when both Guthrie and Guinness arrived in Stratford, they were extremely good about giving interviews and accommodating the press. This was, I think, largely because they had such respect for our head of publicity, Mary Jolliffe.

Guthrie confessed in his letter that, although finances and business were not "in [his] sphere," he hoped that we would not "think it impertinent" if he stated his views on certain matters.

These included "box office" and "publicity-information." Of the former, Tony wrote that "this is a very expert and specialized 'trade.' A good box office manager can make an enormous difference not merely to the good will of the project, but to the financial turnover. 'Packing' and 'dressing' a house demand experience and it simply 'WON'T DO' to think in terms of local volunteers."

In his long letter, Guthrie also expressed some reservations about publicity. "Cecil feels, with great awareness that this is not his sphere [another instance of Tony's near-obsequious desire to not offend], that arrangements in this department are not sufficiently advanced. Are you planning to have an office open in Stratford for enquiries with photographs of leading artists, notes about the plays, etc? And surely by now the material should be ready for Brochures, giving all details, accommodation, catering arrangements and so on."

By this time, of course, Mary Jolliffe, with the help of Jimmy Cowan, was already hard at work on publicity. She was in touch, not only with the local and Toronto press – with whom her ebullience and good-natured charm quickly made her everyone's favourite press agent – but with the foreign press as well. She wrote regularly to such major figures as Brooks Atkinson of *The New York Times* to keep them up to date with plans for the Festival and to stir their curiosity about what was going on in that unheard-of town in that unknown country to the north.

Others also joined in to help, including an ex-Stratford-ian who worked in a Toronto advertising agency and placed ads for us, and a fellow-worker at Maclean Hunter, Chris Yaneff, who designed the first brochure. I think he was paid something like sixty dollars for his efforts. (Yaneff went on to design the internationally admired Commodore computer logo and is now one of the country's premier graphic designers.)

Guthrie concluded his letter with fears about accommodation: "No doubt this has by now been tackled in a big way, but I think I ought to say that my impression in January was that everyone was being a little over-confident about what is potentially one of the main snags." But, by late February, there were committees on both accommodation and catering, and both were progressing well.

Tony's last paragraph was optimistic in the one category

where he should not have been. "I have not alluded at all to the Capital Fund, but we were delighted that you are satisfied with the local response and assume that the substantial promises of outside assistance are now being implemented."

One of the major hopes – and eventual disappointments – had been our application to the Atkinson Foundation of Toronto. On a Thursday morning in May, we got a call from them informing us that two of their people, Norman Folland and his assistant, were down in Stratford. They were settled into a room in the Queen's Hotel.

When I saw them, the first thing they asked was to see our budget. What budget? "The budget," if we could glorify it by the title, had gone from my notepad to a mimeograph sheet, on which countless revisions had been made in pencil. In short, there was no real "budget" for the Stratford Shakespearean Festival, and I could hardly hand a messy sheet of paper over and declare (with suitable Elizabethan flourish), "Here is our budget, sire."

The "budget" was at Alf Bell's home. Alf, the manager of Sealed Power Piston Rings, was the head of our campaign committee. I phoned his home and asked his wife, Dama Bell, who was to become very involved and who served on the Stratford Festival board into the 1980s, "Is Alf around? Can we get the budget?"

"He's out of town today," she replied, as if I were asking to borrow a lawn mower. "I'll look around and see if I can find it."

She was able to find it, so I rushed over, grabbed it and took it back to the office. There, I was greeted by Florence Pelton and Fran Tomkins, who, along with me, made up our total permanent staff in Stratford. Since we had three typewriters in the office, we each took a page and between us typed up a fresh, new budget and took it over to Norman Folland at noon hour. Talk about fly-by-night!

I remained with Folland and his assistant until around five o'clock, answering their detailed questions on every aspect of the Festival. They really did a job on me, and by the time I left I felt like Richard III did after his horse took off. I then went home for dinner, during which I received a call: There was one more financial figure they wanted. I did not know the figure and realized I had to get it from Monty Monteith, a chartered accountant who was in the firm Monteith and Monteith, and who was greatly involved in our whole project.

I knew that, at that hour, his offices were probably closed. But I could not possibly admit that I lacked this important figure. I went to the local bowling alley where I found George Trethaway, a senior partner of Monteith and Monteith, who also did work on the Festival finances (such as they were). He unlocked the accountants' offices and quickly found the needed figure. I took it over to the Queen's Hotel, where I remained talking with my inquisitors until nearly midnight.

The following morning, I received a further call from Norman Folland.

"We would like to see your treasurer."

I knew, because of our financial crisis, that the treasurer, Bill Kalbfleisch, was in a terrible jam. As manager of the local Bank of Montreal, he had stuck his neck out for us, and if the Stratford Festival fell through, his head office was going to hold him responsible. Indeed, he was personally more out on a limb than anybody else. As a result of all this tension, he had, the night before, gone to the Officers' Mess, where he had, let us say, one too many.

I knew that Kalbfleisch was in no condition to talk with these Atkinson guys, so I told them that our treasurer had the flu. They seemed satisfied with this answer and passed to other questions, which, luckily, I was able to answer.

The men from the Atkinson Foundation worked on their report all Friday afternoon, and at eight the next morning they began to phone each member of the Stratford Festival board in turn. They had a number of questions they still wanted answered, but they chose to ask each board member just one question. Their questions were inter-related, so the answers also had to tie together. Their idea was to reach the members of the board before they had any time to collude in their answers. Not that there was much chance of that happening because, in those days in our town, Saturday was truly a day off; a day on which one went to the market or on an outing.

Later, the Atkinson people phoned me and announced, "We're sorry that the treasurer is under the weather, but we are going over to see him."

But Kalbfleisch was still "under the weather." I managed to reach him and told him, "Bill, you are going to *have* to see these guys!"

"Oh God," he moaned. "I just got out of bed. I look awful, and I haven't even shaved yet."

"They understand that you're not well," I told him. "But they are coming over to your house to see you. You just *have* to do it."

They did go over to the treasurer's house, but I never did discover what happened there. Afterwards they returned to their hotel room and wrote their report in rough. They then called a meeting of the board for three o'clock that Saturday afternoon.

This was the beginning of our greatest financial crisis. They read the report to us – which was, incidentally, the first truly objective study that had been done on the Festival to that point – and we all learned a great deal from it. It was a hell of a good one. (For me, it was a real eye-opener. We were so enthusiastic about the entire project that we usually stumbled from day to day, often forgetting to pick up the loose ends which had to be tied. I was always worrying about what might happen tomorrow, and here was a professional report that said that there was this and that and the other thing which we *had* to look after.) It concluded: "We therefore will recommend to the Atkinson Foundation that X thousand dollars [sic] be given to the Stratford Festival."

Folland then looked at us and declared, "Now, you realize that this creates a crisis. Because we can't give you money unless we are guaranteed that the Festival will go ahead. Therefore, we have to give you enough money that you can give us the guarantee that it will go ahead. How much?"

(Some background here, since, to coin a phrase, men, and foundations, are political animals. The Atkinson Foundation had been set up as a charitable institution by *The Toronto*

Star. The wealthy, left-leaning newspaper was strongly opposed to the Conservative provincial government of Leslie Frost. Frost, in turn, often accused them of setting up the Atkinson Foundation to avoid taxes. So there were a number of political tensions which had nothing to do with the Stratford Festival, but everything to do with whether or not we would get the money.)

A number of people on the board were thinking along the line of "We've got them in a hole! They *have* to give some money away to a good cause. They will offer us the money for political reasons."

So they declared, "We need fifty thousand dollars."

Folland replied, "How about twenty-five?"

To which some of the board responded, "No, we can't do it with twenty-five grand; we need fifty."

I saw that there was some opposition to this position of holding out for the most money, so I offered a compromise: "Can we split the difference and make it thirty-five thousand?"

"No! It has to be fifty" insisted a number of the board members, led by a very strong conservative.

Folland finally said, "Okay. We'll recommend fifty thousand dollars to the Atkinson Foundation. You have a meeting of your board at three on Monday afternoon, and we'll have an answer for you then. We realize that you are under great pressure, so we'll meet with the head of the Foundation at his home tomorrow morning, and we'll have a meeting of our board this very evening."

So that was it! (Or so it seemed). We appeared to have our fifty thousand in the bag, and everyone was happy.

I was even happier than most because of some top-secret negotiations with Governor General Vincent Massey. All during this time, I had been in touch with the Governor General through Lionel Massey, his son and executive assistant. That day, the Governor General was on his way out to Victoria to preside over the Dominion Drama Festival. The younger Massey, who was accompanying him, phoned me from his home early in the morning, then from a train in Union Station in Toronto, and again from the Winnipeg airport to find out what was happening. Finally, shortly after five that afternoon, just after I had returned from the board meeting, Lionel called me once again, this time from Victoria. (There were no direct flights across the country at that time.)

"How did the meeting go?" he asked me.

"It looks as if we got fifty thousand dollars from Atkinson!" I exclaimed.

"Count us in for another ten," he said, on behalf of the Masseys. No one was to know about their generosity – it had to be kept strictly confidential. But I knew we now had sixty thousand dollars!

The letter and the cheque from the Massey Foundation arrived on the first of June, and the former is a precious document in the Stratford Archives today. Labelled "PER-SONAL & CONFIDENTIAL," it declared that the Governor General would be "delighted to receive Dr. Harry Showalter and yourself" on June 11.

"I am more than glad to hear that everything is progressing so well and I know it will be a great event, in fact, unique, in Canada," wrote his son and secretary, Lionel Massey. Then he got to the good part: "I am making arrangements for a cheque for $10,000 to be sent to you by the National Trust Company as a contribution to the Festival from the Massey Foundation." And note the delicacy of his final words: "I know you will understand how very, very important it is that this should remain completely anonymous. It would be most embarrassing to the Trustees of the Foundation if such information should get into the press because so many other organizations would be writing in for grants." In other words, if the other kids see you get the ice cream, they'll all start demanding some, too.

But it was all too good to be true. While I was dreaming in technicolor about the $10,000 from the Masseys, and the $50,000 from the Atkinsons, little did I know that we were being hoisted on our own petard, to coin a phrase. We had forgotten that our largest single donation until that time had been for $5,000, which made our request for $50,000 really quite outlandish, even impossible. In other words, because of the sensitive political situation between the Foundation and the Premier of Ontario, it would have been outrageous for Atkinson to give the Stratford Festival *ten times* our previous largest donation; they could so easily be accused of dumping a large sum to avoid taxes. And so, the day following our meeting with the Atkinson Foundation people, Sunday May 11, I received a phone call from Harry Showalter. "I've got bad news for you, Tom. The Atkinson Foundation has turned us down."

"Completely?" I choked.

"Completely," he replied. It was helpful that he was the superintendent of the Baptist Sunday School and a deeply religious man, because the following words from his lips were much sweeter than most of ours would have been. As the entire Stratford Shakespearean Festival appeared to be crashing down around us, Showalter whispered, *"Golly, Tom!"*

That was one of the first beautiful days in May, and Showalter had been working like mad for months on our project, so I understood when he said, "Tom, I promised my kids that I would take them for a drive today, and I just can't get out of it again!"

"Harry," I said, "You get the hell out of town, and don't tell anybody about this, because there's no time for a board meeting! If it all falls apart, then blame it on me. But it's got to be that way."

"Okay," Harry replied. And he left town without telling a soul.

I then went to see Monty Monteith, that same Sunday afternoon. Monty Monteith's father-in-law was the head of the Perth Mutual Insurance Company – a very wealthy man. As I walked in, Monty said to me, "I've got a great idea, Tom. Now that an out-of-town organization is giving us fifty thousand, it should be a local one to give us twenty-five thousand. So I'm going to the Old Man!" (Meaning his rich in-law, Harry Strudley.)

Monty did not know about the Massey Foundation money, but neither did he know the awful news from the Atkinson Foundation.

"I think you're going to have to change that, Monty," I told him. "We've just lost the fifty grand from Atkinson."

Our first move was to phone every wealthy man and woman

we knew in Canada and some we did not know. We did not know Sam Bronfman, but we called the owner of Seagram's that same Sunday afternoon, and stated, "We need twenty-five thousand by tomorrow morning!"

"What are you calling *me* for??" the multi-millionaire asked.

"Well," I stammered, "you've got this distillery in Kitchener, and that's pretty near here. . . ."

"*But whisky has nothing to do with Shakespeare!*" he boomed.

We finally realized that all this was getting us nowhere, and in no great hurry, either. For the longest time we sat around, like men trying to put off their execution, and had a few drinks. Finally, Monty Monteith lept up.

"Goddammit, Tom!" (He was not religious.) "I'll sell him on the idea that if an out-of-town organization turned us down, then it's up to a local one to save us!"

At that time, the father-in-law of Monty Monteith was in his late seventies; getting old, but still extremely active. There was a group of men like himself in Stratford, all old natives of the city, who used to walk to work every morning. The man was in the habit of walking with one of his friends in particular, a fellow director of Perth Mutual. Monty was concerned that if his father-in-law met his friend on the way to work the next day, his friend would talk him out of any donation to the Stratford Festival.

So Monty got up early the next morning and waited in his car in front of his father-in-law's house. His purpose was clear: to pick the old man up and drive him to work, so that he would have no chance to meet his friend on the way!

The old man agreed to take Monty's proposal to his executive. Because all the directors of the company were local Stratford people, they were able to organize a meeting for that same lunchtime. The only snag the executive saw was that their company was a mutual insurance company, which meant that they would be giving away their mutual shareholder's money. Twenty-five thousand dollars was too big an amount for them simply to charge to advertising or some similar account. I was later told that they actually phoned the Inspector of Insurance in Ottawa and asked "What'll happen if. . .?"

They were told, "Well, if nobody complains, I'm not going to."

Monty Monteith sat outside while the insurance company had its board meeting. A short time later, the Festival board members gathered in the Festival office to hear what they expected to be good news from Atkinson.

At ten minutes to three, Monty rushed into my office, and by the smile on his face, I knew that he had been successful.

We called the meeting of the Stratford Festival board to order, and Harry Showalter got up and declared, "I'm very sorry to have to announce that we were not successful in getting the fifty thousand from the Atkinson Foundation. [Gasps] But in the meantime, we have received two anonymous donations: One of ten thousand dollars [from the Massey Foundation] and one of twenty-five thousand [from the Perth Mutual Insurance Company]. Now, do we go ahead, or don't we?"

And everyone cried out, "Go!"

The first thing I did after that "Go!" was to phone Oliver Gaffney. Gaffney greeted the news with his normal equanimity. He was not the kind of man who ever got excited, ecstatic, or depressed. (In like manner, whenever Harry Showalter was troubled, he would head off to the church and play the organ to soothe his nerves and soul. A lot of psychiatrists would be unemployed if more people acted like some of our small-town men and women). Oliver Gaffney did so much with absolutely no fuss, never asking such uncomfortable questions as "When the hell am I going to get my money?" He just went ahead and did what he had to do; or rather, what we needed him to do. Later the president of the Stratford Festival, he was and is a marvellous man.

Nearly one half of the original money for our project was given by the people and businesses of Stratford. Their effort was quite remarkable, but, in my opinion, they have never received the praise they deserved. The eventual amount we raised was the magnificent sum of $157,000 including, ironically, ten thousand dollars from the Atkinson Foundation, which arrived late in the campaign. With this money, plus the revenue from the box (ticket sales were extraordinary, right from the start), we managed to pay for the tent and theatre construction, the "star" English contingent, a company of sixty-four Canadian performers, the mounting of two major Shakespearean productions, and to come out of a six-week season with a mere $4,270 deficit.

Not bad, for a bunch of small-town impresarios.

10

Props from Mops
and Other Inventions

SHOWALTER=
 STRATFORD ONTARIO

CONFIRMING CONVERSATION MUST HAVE FIRM DECISION
WHETHER FESTIVAL PROCEEDING STOP GUINNESS HAVING
BOOKED SAIL TUESDAY MORNING WOULD WELCOME EARLIEST
DECISION HUMANLY POSSIBLE STOP ALL REGRET NECESSITY
COMPEL IMMEDIATE DECISION STOP IN VIEW MY INTENSE
PREOCCUPATION OLD VIC PLEASE CABLE OR TELEPHONE
GUINNESS LONDON RIVERSIDE 5542=

 GUTHRIE

This telegram, now in the Stratford archives, was sent on May 2, 1953. Harry Showalter read it and immediately telephoned Alec in London. Harry admitted that the situation was pretty desperate, but that the board was "determined to go ahead," because of the good prospects for donations. In one of his many magnanimous gestures, Guinness replied that he had to leave on the boat for New York within a few days, and if we *did* decide to cancel before he left, he would not hold us to his contract, which, in any case, was not yet signed.

Guinness added, however, that if our decision – whichever way it went – was made while he was in passage, he would appreciate being informed before he got off the boat in New York, so that he would know what to say before he had to talk to reporters. That's the kind of man he was. And is.

As you can see, the news of our financial problems had reached the Old Country, although all's well that ends well. But before it ended well, we all lived with constant tension and near-heartbreak, as can be seen in the minutes of the meetings of the Stratford board that spring. On April 30, 1952, the finance chairman, Alf Bell, claimed that the board was "convinced the money was still there and it could be reached, but that time was running short and since a business isn't run on wishful thinking, steps had to be taken to contact a professional money raiser for charities who was willing to take on our project without having positive direction from Stratford." (It is interesting to note that professional fund-raisers *were* approached, but none was found to be any more capable than we amateurs.)

There was even a motion for postponement at that meeting, which was made just before the dismaying news from Atkinson Foundation was announced. I spoke passionately against it. "Mr. Patterson asked the Foundation to have faith in the festival," the minutes read. "It had taken courage to get as far as we had and he asked for courage to keep it going. As most of the actors, actresses, directors and designers were proverbially temperamental, this must be taken into account, as we could not replace them at this date. Any mention of a postponement, even for a week, would upset the apple cart."

When the motion arose, it was from a man who was slurring his words badly. I suspected that there might be a clique pushing for the postponement, so I jotted down notes and passed one to each member, asking "how can you vote on this motion when the man is in this condition?" Their backs went up, and when he finished talking, they attacked him. They finally decided to postpone the motion of postponement to give the presenter time to sober up! The motion never came up again. Alcohol was the saviour of many moments in the history of the Stratford Festival.

Once again we were firm in our resolve to continue, and as soon as the director and star were calmed, and were on their way to Canada, I returned to the one thousand and one other things we had to take care of.

We had initially projected a four-week season of two plays. But even before we opened in mid-July, the ticket sales were so great that we decided to extend the Festival for another two weeks.

One of our first moves was to make out a seating plan and have tickets printed. But what to charge? And that, I must admit, is one of the more charming stories of the "professionalism" of the fledgling Stratford Festival.

We knew we could not take on ticket sales ourselves, so we lined up a travel agency in Toronto, University Tours, to sell them for us. Its owner, Ken Conn, agreed to do this, but we had no price for the tickets!

"If I'm going to handle this," Conn told me, "then you've got to know by this afternoon. Otherwise, I'm not taking the project on."

So Cecil Clarke and I went to downtown Toronto and bought a *New York Times* and looked through its entertainment section. After scouring all the ads, we found the theatre which charged the highest prices. Those became our prices. This is known as scientific entrepreneurship. Lovers of trivia (and haters of inflation) will be interested (and horrified) to learn that the prices for seats at the first Stratford Festival were $6.00, $5.00, $4.00, $3.00, $1.80, and $1.00. (It should be noted that a single copy of *Maclean's* magazine during that year cost fifteen cents, a year's subscription, $3.00. So as one can quickly see, the cost of going to the theatre has increased far less than the price of a magazine.)

Normally, deciding on such matters as ticket prices would be done by a committee, with accountants to calculate how much to charge per seat in order to cover costs. But in 1953, our "professional" approach was simply to cut out the advertisement from the *Times*, bring it to the travel agent, and tell him, "That's your price list!"

The ticket agent was a very volatile man and, I must admit, far more temperamental than any of the actors I had met to that date. He wanted an advertising budget of ten thousand dollars. I can not now recall what our budget was for this item, or even if we had allotted anything at all. But when I brought up the subject with the board, they were willing to put only five thousand dollars aside. When I reported this to Conn, he went into a real flap and threatened to throw all our nice, new tickets right out his third-floor window.

Cecil and I met again with members of the board, but they were adamant – just as adamant as our agent. (Although they did not recommend throwing *him* out the window.) So the morning after this meeting, I checked with a lawyer and was told that a telegram is not a legal document – at least that is what I was told. So Florence Pelton and I sent Ken Conn of University Tours a telegram authorizing him to spend the full ten thousand, and he was happy. I was not ashamed at all, either.

None of us had realized just how popular this Festival was going to be – including Ken Conn, the travel agent-cum-ticket seller. Conn's third-floor office was in a building at the corner of Carlton and Yonge streets in downtown Toronto, and his entire staff was two or three people who organized trips to Europe. But as soon as Festival tickets were offered to the public, there were people lining up for them in front of his desk, down three flights of stairs, right down to Yonge Street, and around the corner on to Carlton. In other words, Conn found himself selling five- and six-dollar tickets to the Stratford Festival, while people who wanted to fly off on expensive vacations were unable to get near his office. He was furious. (True, he got a nominal commission for selling the tickets, and he had sold around 60 per cent of the house before we opened. But European trips are somewhat more costly than theatre tickets for Shakespearean productions, unless you are including a trip to Stratford-upon-Avon in the price.)

We never figured out our exact break-even point, nor how much of our total costs would be covered by ticket sales, as we were never out to make money. All we knew was that we had budgeted for $150,000 in donations, and had received, even before the season ended, $157,000. Our ticket sales brought in around $150,000, which allowed us to do the whole damned thing, as noted, with a final deficit of less than $4,300. (I am repeating myself, I know, but I am still proud of it.)

Meanwhile the building was causing us other problems. Although slightly out of chronological order, it is worth noting here what happened when Alec Guinness gave his first soliloquy in front of the entire company when rehearsals finally started in the tent, shortly before opening night. He stood on stage and started out with the opening lines of *Richard III*, "Now is the winter of our discontent. . . ." And it was immediately obvious that the discontent would be that summer, as well. You could not hear a single one of his words! They simply bounced off the bare concrete bowl and vanished into space.

Panic quickly set in as the cheerful mood of the company abruptly collapsed. We were sitting in a big, white elephant, which looked pretty good, but clearly was not going to work! There was considerable discussion along the lines of "Maybe when the audience is all seated, their bodies would soak up. . . ." Indeed, we came up with the idea of inviting hundreds of Stratford people to a rehearsal to see if their bodies would absorb the echo. But then we realized that if we did this, and it did not succeed, there would be around fifteen hundred souls who might spread the word that this whole structure was a very pretty, but nonetheless very white elephant.

Then Guthrie came up with the answer. "What we need is some kind of material to cover the concrete," he declared. So off to the rescue went our hero, Oliver Gaffney. He had jobs all over the province, including bridge construction, and so he went everywhere, dragging huge tarps off his partially-completed projects. He brought them in, and we spread the tarps over the concrete. (By this time, we had worked out a schedule: Gaffney would work on the theatre building at night, while the company rehearsed by day.) Each night, he spread more of the tarps out, so there would be two tarps across the concrete one morning, two more the next, until the concrete was all covered. The tent was up, but, luckily, the seats had not yet been installed.

Eventually, we discovered that the quickest way of solving the problem – and also, not coincidentally, the cheapest – was to cover the concrete with coco-matting. We searched the country for the material and found that there were only two companies in all of Canada that made the material in the bastard size needed, one in Moose Jaw, Saskatchewan, as I recall; the other in Port Credit, Ontario.

It was here that Eaton's, the department store chain, stepped in. (Eaton's had already given us some financial support and had helped to line up material for wardrobe.) We phoned our man at Eaton's, Jack Brockie, and told him, "We need lots of coco-matting, and in a bastard size, to fit over the concrete steps."

"I'll see what I can do," Brockie replied. He phoned the company in nearby Port Credit, had them cut the matting to the size we needed, and sent Eaton's trucks to the firm. As the material piled off the assembly lines, it was rolled into the trucks, which carted it to Stratford.

Then we lined up a number of staple guns that can fire into concrete, and some members of the board actually came down and laid the material; really quite a remarkable operation. When the rehearsals ended each evening, we would pull one tarp off, staple down some coco-matting, and so continue into the night, until we finished. We were all immensely relieved when we finally heard for ourselves the considerable improvement the matting made to the tent's acoustic quality.

But that spring, we were too busy with fundraising, hiring, and a hundred other details to worry much about the theatre itself. The tent had been ordered from a Chicago manufacturer, and Gaffney was working flat out on construction – things seemed to be under control. We turned our attention to wardrobe and property.

The wardrobe, of course, was designed by Tanya Moiseiwitsch. Before Ray Diffen arrived from Stratford-upon-Avon and began work on the costumes, Tanya's sketches of her designs for *Richard III* were displayed by the Royal Ontario

Museum in Toronto – another example of the help we were given in publicizing the Festival.

The assistant Ray Diffen had chosen to accompany him to Stratford in place of my future wife was the flamboyant Londoner and skilled cutter, Annette Geber. Annette always wore a lot of make-up and her hair-do, which would pass for normal in today's fashions, was, in 1953, quite outrageous. We quickly found out that her talent and her taste in period costuming were just as impressive as her looks.

Through the kind offer of Dora Mavor Moore, Diffen and Geber organized, from scratch, a wardrobe department in the New Play Society's rehearsal hall in Toronto. With the help of a team of Canadians, who had little experience, if any, in creating costumes, they produced a wardrobe that became the talk of the North American theatre world. Their level of skill set a new standard, not only for the Festival but for the whole Canadian theatre scene. The Canadians who were trained by Diffen and Geber can now be found in the wardrobe departments of major cultural institutions around the world – the New York Metropolitan Opera, the Royal Ballet in London, England, and in Stratford-upon-Avon, to name just a few.

One wardrobe problem that caused Cecil Clarke some concern was the matter of footwear for the actors. Some special boots had been ordered from England, but we still needed shoes. He had visited some of the largest shoe manufacturers in the province, but none had been the slightest interested in creating a few dozen shoes for a couple of Shakespearean plays.

At long last, he somehow tracked down a shoemaker, a Jewish refugee from Eastern Europe, who was an old-fashioned craftsman of the kind rarely found today. The way he would sit in the back corner of his little shop in Toronto's garment district with his leather and work away reminded me of the character Gepetto in *Pinocchio*. His firm, the Snug-Fit Shoe Company, was set up to make shoes for industrial plants, but it did not take Cecil long to kindle the shoemaker's interest.

"Here are the designs," Cecil told him. "These have to

be like – well, *Richard III* goes back to the fifteenth century in England." And the old shoemaker, who seemed to be bored with his growing business of making felt shoes, just went wild. He studied the designs, then he and his sons (who handled the business for him) went off to the Royal Ontario Museum to research the footwear of the period. He became truly creative, and loved the work. We eventually had everyone's shoe size, so each pair was made to fit each actor. The shoemaker crafted hundreds of pairs, each different, loaded them up in the back of his car, and drove them to Stratford.

Clarke also found a marvellous hat maker, Lily Jamon, who was originally from France but was now living in Toronto making high-fashion hats. Suddenly, she found herself with the task of making fifteenth and sixteenth century headwear.

Although Cecil Clarke was an extraordinary organizer, some of the finding of craftspeople was done rather *ad hoc*. The hat maker, for example, applied for the job after reading about the upcoming Festival in the newspapers. But most commissions were carefully planned by Cecil. He went to the local Stratford tinsmith at Kincaid's Metal Shop, who normally made pipes for furnaces, and showed him how to refine his craft and make shields for medieval soldiers. Each shield used by our company was made, to specifications, by this Stratford tinsmith.

At the same time that Diffen and Geber were organizing the wardrobe in Toronto, Cecil Clarke was setting up a property department in Stratford. Most of us on the board were happily ignorant of the exacting requirements involved in the finding and making of props. We were under the impression that if we needed an old chair, well, "Aunt Matilda has a nice old chair in her basement we can borrow." We simply did not see the anachronism of using a Victorian chair in a fifteenth century play. What did it matter? It was old, was it not? We had thought that a committee could take care of props by scrounging pieces from friends, relatives, and storekeepers. At most, we anticipated borrowing items from antique shops in exchange for a credit line in the program.

Cecil soon set us straight. We had to have a property department; we had to use props that were true to the time period of the play. So we hired Jacqueline Cundall, Cecil's wife, as head of the property department. There were, I am sure, eyebrows raised at the apparent nepotism of this appointment. But Jacqueline, a quiet, even demure young woman, rapidly proved her considerable talent.

Soon after her arrival, Cundall hired a team of aspiring artists and artisans, whose applications for work in our property department had poured in from across Canada. They formed a remarkably creative team, who set a standard for properties at Stratford that remains unparallelled in North America.

Thanks to the kindness of Len Webster, president of the local O'Cedar Mop Company and later a member of the Festival board, the property department was set up in an unused section of his factory. The O'Cedar Mop factory was overflowing with the cellular material that they made the mops from. Every night, the night watchman-cum-janitor swept out the factory, gathering all the unused pieces of material to throw out. These odds and ends were like sponge, but stronger, as they were cellulose.

It took only a few days for the imaginative property workers to realize that this so-called garbage was a gold mine. They made a deal with the janitor that he would not dispose of this material until they had a chance to go through it. Out of the "garbage" they picked pieces of cellulose, which ended up as decorations on armour, shields, hats, and anything else that needed embellishment.

Once, when a toilet in the factory broke down and had to be replaced, this imaginative team retrieved the float and, with the application of glue, paint, and some O'Cedar Mop sweepings, transformed it into Richard III's orb of office.

Similar stories abound. At one point, we realized that we had need of a bath-chair for Alec Guinness in *All's Well That Ends Well*, in which he would play the cameo role of the King of France. (Alec had refused to star in both plays, agreeing with Guthrie that it was enough that he would dominate the stage in *Richard III*; they both wanted to allow the Canadian performers a chance to shine.) We got *The Globe and Mail* to run a story about our problem, and – surprise – someone wrote in to say that they had a bath-chair they were willing to lend to the Festival.

Some ideas for props came from the master director himself. Tony had decided to open the first play of the Festival in as dramatic a manner as possible. He wanted a bell to toll before Alec Guinness walked on stage to deliver the opening lines of *Richard III*. We checked around and discovered that there was a bell-maker, Carl Stoermer, just outside Kitchener, not far from Stratford. The craftsman had come from a village in Czechoslovakia – a community where, apparently, everyone made bells. (In Canada, this would be called a one-industry town, and is not recommended.)

We went to visit Stoermer in his shop on the outskirts of the city. There were bells everywhere! His door-bell was not an electric contraption that you pushed; it was a brass bell that you pulled. And in front of his tiny house there was a stand, about ten feet square and fifteen to twenty feet high, in which hung a massive brass bell that weighed probably two or three tons.

Carl Stoermer was kind enough to lend the bell to Clarke. It became such a part of the Festival that, after the first year, a group of people banded together and insisted that we should not return the bell to Stoermer, but should purchase it from him. They were able to raise enough money. To this day, the bell hangs in the Stratford Festival theatre.

11

Rehearsals Begin

Back in the early 1950s in Canada, Actors' Equity and ACTRA did not exist, and there appeared no real reason that they should. There was little professional theatre in the country, and most actors worked for CBC Radio. Dora Mavor Moore never had much money to pay her performers, most of whom were making a semi-living over at the Corporation, anyway. So there was no fixed wage rate for actors, and we had no idea what to pay our performers.

A number of the actors we had approached got together and decided that, "if this is professional theatre at Stratford this summer, then we're going to have to get paid." And if and when we would insist that it was "*such* a great honour to work with Tyrone Guthrie and Alec Guinness," they agreed to retort that the honour was not good enough; that they *wanted to be paid*.

So, apparently, these performers decided among themselves a schedule of fees, for less than which they would not act. The problem was, we did not know that they had done this. What we had devised was simple, if crude: We picked four people whose roles were of differing levels of difficulty. This had nothing to do with their reputations as actors, but it helped us to figure out what we would suggest to them as payment. Among the actors chosen in each of these "acting divisions" were Eric House and Bill Needles, both of whom would become perennial favourites at the Festival.

The performers came in to talk money with, we assumed, a bit of a chip on their collective shoulders. Sure there was all this drama and excitement about a Shakespearean Festival in Canada – but *how much are you paying*?

As each actor came in, Cecil Clarke would say to him or her, "We understand that you would like to be a member of the company. There will be six weeks of rehearsal and six weeks of acting."

We told each actor what they would require, and we discussed accommodations. Then we asked them what they thought they should receive for the twelve weeks' work.

Interestingly, in every single case but one, the figure we had reached was either identical to the fee demanded or actually above it! The fee was around $600 for the season – not bad wages for the time.

I recall one rather funny moment. One performer mentioned money, and Cecil Clarke jumped to a question about *All's Well*, which was to be performed in modern dress: "Do you have a tux?"

"Look," said the actor, "let's get back to payment. What's it going to be?"

And Cecil replied, "What you mentioned before. . . . Isn't that satisfactory? We accept that, and think it's fine."

The one case that differed has its own charm. When it was Bill Needles's turn to negotiate with us, he asked for less money than we had agreed to give him, and we accepted his (lower) suggestion. Then, after we got through this rather strenuous exercise, Cecil and I looked at each other, without even mentioning Bill's name.

"We can't do it, can we?" said Cecil, somewhat cryptically.

"No, we can't" I replied, knowing that it would throw off everyone, and we did not want to create bad feelings later about the variance in payment.

So that evening, I phoned Bill Needles. I couldn't resist teasing him a little, because I knew full well that most of the performers had come into negotiations with chips on their shoulders.

Bill's wife answered and told me that he was out.

"It's Tom Patterson. Would you please have Bill phone me when he's back?"

A while later, Needles returned my call.

"Yeah? What do you want?"

"Well, Bill, I'm sorry, but we made a terrible mistake when we were negotiating your fee," I told him, my voice dripping with evil glee.

"Oh?" he asked, his voice concerned, almost angry.

"Yes. We want to offer you a hundred dollars more."

"*What!*" he cried.

And that set the pattern for the rest of the company. The only actors who received anything near Guinness's fee were Irene Worth and Douglas Campbell. Guinness had insisted on receiving at least $100 more than anyone else, and we stuck to that agreement.

Early in 1953, we set up a committee to work on finding accommodation for the performers. This was hooked in with our ever-nervous campaign to raise money, of course. One of the ways that we decided to impress people with the fact that a lot of money was pouring in, was to take out an ad in *The Beacon-Herald* asking Stratfordians if they had any spare rooms. Please write in, we asked them; we are anticipating a huge demand for lodgings from the actors and, later, from theatre-goers.

We were scared stiff. We were terrified that every fast-buck artist in town would soon be knocking at the Festival's doors, to make their fortune out of lodging visitors. Today, we can tell Stratfordians "your home is not suitable for guests." But back then, we could not risk further antagonizing the people who were against the Festival by saying something like that.

Fortunately, none of the nay-sayers offered their homes. So we ended up obtaining rooms in the homes of Stratford's most supportive and generous residents. The performers thought that they would be staying in tourist homes. But no – they were guesting!

That was one of our smartest moves. Right from the beginning, we decided that we would not call anyone a "tourist." They were, rather, "Festival guests." All our advertising read that it was our obligation to look after "our Festival guests." And this created the attitude among Stratford people that "These people are our guests. We've got to look after them." This, rather than "make a fast buck out of them."

Furthermore, when the actors poured into town in late May, they quickly realized that here was a great situation! They were staying in the types of homes where the owners would wait up at night for the performers to get home from rehearsals, and give them coffee or drinks. This atmosphere was essential to the success of the entire Festival. (It is interesting to note that this attitude still exists today. Whereas most towns today have a "Tourist Bureau," in Stratford, we have a "Visitors and Convention Bureau.")

While the whole of Stratford was becoming deeply involved with "this Festival thing," very few of its citizens knew anything about Shakespeare, let alone his plays. So a determined woman, Mrs. John Adamson, decided to correct this situation single-handedly. She was a one-time teacher of English who had retired when she married my former chemistry teacher at the Collegiate Institute. Until the time of the Festival, I do not think many people even knew of her existence.

But the Festival gave her the opportunity to blossom. She organized a Shakespearean study group to teach the two plays chosen for that first season, and her success was quite phenomenal – leading Stratford socialites and wives of prominent businessmen all attended the study group faithfully.

Mrs. Adamson – a school teacher of the Old School – conducted her classes like the traditional Victorian schoolmistress: with homework, tests, and more. And all her "students" accepted this.

Alas, her interpretation of Shakespeare left something to be desired. It was apparently based on Victorian morality, and was heavily bowdlerized. Guthrie, after reading a story in *The Beacon-Herald* about the remarkable Mrs. Adamson and her remedial work with our citizens, was greatly tempted to criticize what she was doing. When the great director realized more fully the effort and good will that Mrs. Adamson and her pupils were putting into this studious effort, he refrained from negative comment. But it was not easy for him to do so!

Rehearsals for the first Stratford Festival season were to begin in early June, exactly six weeks before our opening on July 13, 1953. Alec Guinness had come over about six weeks early, which we really appreciated, because some people had doubted that he would ever come.

He arrived early for a number of reasons. He had nothing else going on since he had turned down that film in order to come to Stratford. Furthermore, he wanted to go fishing. Let me allow him to tell it in his own, delightful way, as he did in his best-selling memoirs, *Blessings in Disguise*.

When I arrived in Canada, two weeks ahead of the rehearsal schedule, the theatre was just a muddy hole in the ground about six feet deep and ten feet square. It didn't look promising. Tony and I gazed at it with foreboding; then he said, "Rise above it." Not a difficult feat, physically. "Rise above it" was his catch-phrase for anything tiresome, undesirable or even disastrous, from undrinkable, tepid, canteen coffee, to toothache, or to the loss of all costumes and scenery on tour. Having arrived early in order to familiarise myself with my surroundings, and with time on my hands, I accepted an invitation from three delightful young Canadians to go on a canoeing and fishing expedition, for ten days, up the French River. When not engaged in back-breaking portage round waterfalls and rapids, batting off mosquitoes, avoiding poison ivy, heroically paddling a canoe or casting a line for muskalonge – a sort of large game pike – I tried to learn my lines, to the round-eyed astonishment of my companions, who were not used to muttering actors. It was one of the most spectacular and enjoyable holidays I've ever had and I returned to Stratford fit and fairly trim, only to find the theatre had barely progressed. However, Cecil Clarke, who was our English manager, had done wonders of organisation and a mock-up replica of the stage we would be using had been housed in a barn-like disused warehouse with a tin roof, on which the rain thundered, drowning the loudest human voices. Also Tanya was busy in the wardrobe's workrooms and beautiful garments were beginning to appear on the tailors' dummies. There was an air of bustle, and striding through it all, clicking his fingers, issuing orders, answering queries, was that tall military figure. And then the entire company took to bicycling and Tony's rehearsals.

It was fascinating to see the great Tyrone Guthrie manipulating a large company of whom he knew half a dozen, had met half a dozen more, and to whom the rest were strangers. He won their hearts and adoring confidence in an hour; made them laugh, made them jump with activity and held them all in the palm of his hand, including myself, who had been in eight previous productions of his and was familiar with his ways.

The entire cast came in on the Sunday before the rehearsals were to begin. We held a reception for the company to meet the people of Stratford, because, once again, this was very much a community affair. Everybody from the city of Stratford was invited, and the gathering took place on the lawn of the Teacher's College, in front of the theatre construction site. Guthrie was there, as well as Alec Guinness and Irene Worth, and they all stood in the receiving line greeting everyone from the city who came. The only drinks served were those made by Harry Showalter's Orange Kist company – of the very soft drink variety, I assure you.

The reception was a great success, and not only for the townspeople, who were finally getting a chance to meet the performers. It was a great success for the actors themselves, who made many friends. Of course, a number of those who were at the reception were "landlords" and had already met their unusual "guests."

The theatre, as Guinness noted, was far from complete. (This, in spite of a promise, as Guinness writes, "that we wouldn't be required to open before we had had three weeks' rehearsal in the completed theatre, and we had a clause to that effect written into our contracts. That clause proved useless; the theatre wasn't ready for our occupation until a week or two before the first night, for which tickets had been sold well in advance.") Nor was the tent up. So Oliver Gaffney, bless his constructive soul, built the replica of the stage in a big barn at the fairgrounds.

That Monday morning, the entire company met for a read-through of the play. The press was everywhere, but it was excluded. After a brief ten minutes at the start of the day – out, out, out.

All the performers had copies of the plays and everything else they needed. What we had not taken into account was that this was the season when the birds' eggs hatch. The roof of the barn was filled with, let us say, mating sparrows. And this, for the next three or four weeks, was where the rehearsals took place. Eggs kept dropping down on the actors' books, the birds kept shitting on everybody, and the occasional baby bird fell from its nest. Surely a sign of fecundity for the festival. (I am old enough to remember hearing that it used to be dissatisfied *patrons* who threw eggs at performers!)

After each of these rather messy rehearsals, the whole company would come down to the park to see how the theatre was coming along. We were now a little over a month before opening. Construction was not going very well, and much of the reason was money – or rather, the eternal, infernal lack of it. To give you an idea of how late we were running, the letter of agreement between the United States Tent & Awning Company of Chicago was dated May 29, 1953 – just days before rehearsals were to begin, and barely six weeks before Alec Guinness was to sweep across the stage as Richard III. In that letter, astonishingly, the supplier agreed to have all the "component parts" (tent quarter poles, wall poles, stakes, tent top, outside wall, inside wall, rigging, hardware fittings, and so on) arrive in Stratford (via Gloversville, New York), "as near as possible to June 20, 1953." (Yes, just *three weeks* before our winter – and possible summer – of discontent was to begin.) Furthermore, we agreed in that rather late contract to pay $10,000 on signing, and the balance of $7,774 when all the parts were ready for shipment.

So the tent had been ordered – weeks late – but we did not have the money to pay for it! It was a gigantic tent; not something that one could pull out from the stock, as if for a backyard party or wedding. It had to be designed specifically to fit the contour of that particular piece of land. No circus tent could be purchased quickly and put up over the theatre. As well, it had to be dyed a certain colour, which had been chosen by Tanya. At one point the tent manufacturer stopped working because our cheques were not forthcoming – or even fifthcoming.

Alf Bell headed up a committee of the board, which was sent down to Chicago to try and talk the United States Tent & Awning Company into allowing our Show To Go On. They were successful. I was back in Stratford, so I was not fully aware of how they managed to convince the tent-makers to resume work, but I believe that they had at least some of the money when they went down to the Windy City.

The tent finally arrived, but hardly when we should have had it. The June 15, 1953, board minutes state that "the tent will be ready for shipping on Wednesday." Then we had to get a tent-master fast, because we had not yet been able to find anybody who knew how to put up a tent the size of the one we had ordered.

Then, thank the Good Lord, Skip Manley, tent master extraordinaire, arrived. He was a fantastic character, and no mere circus man. Guthrie nicknamed him "The Toscanini of tent-makers," because of the way he used his arms and body to "conduct" his workers. But he was more than just a Toscanini; there was a lot of Einstein – and maybe P.T. Barnum – in that man, as well. He had put up Chataqua tents across the United States and had handled religious rallies for the likes of Oral Roberts. He must have been in his late forties then and living in Chicago, which is why the United States Tent & Awning Company recommended him – that, and the fact that he may have been the greatest "tent master" on this planet. He stayed in Stratford throughout the first season, and became one of the heroes of the Festival.

But in the meantime, it was crisis time again: Will the tent ever be up in time? The members of the acting company kept complaining, "We *have* to get on that stage, or we'll never be ready!" Finally, without my knowledge, Alec Guinness wrote a letter to Harry Showalter. In the letter, written on a Thursday, Alec warned that if he and the company did not have at least the assurance that they would be in the theatre by that weekend then he was going to catch the Monday boat back to England. He had checked when the boat was leaving, and listed the times in his letter.

Later that same day, I was driving to the theatre and saw Alec Guinness bicycling on the same route. I stopped the car to talk with him, and he told me, "Oh, by the way, Tom. I wrote a letter to Showalter, saying that I'm going home on Monday."

Then, with a grin on his face, he quickly added, "I thought that it would be a bit of a push to get things moving faster!"

Guinness had had no intention whatsoever of going.

Not that poor Harry Showalter was aware of that fact. I have since read his letter to Alec, dated June 22, 1953, – with a copy sent to Tony Guthrie – and one can almost feel the president of the Shakespearean Festival Foundation shaking in his boots as he dictated it. "Adopting your method of sending notes, I should like to report back on the regrettable problem of the readiness of the theatre. . . ." Showalter then went on to promise a theatre "ready for rehearsals" by June 28 (sixteen days before opening night), and complete dress rehearsal arrangements, "including lighting, painting, etc., will be ready in ample time, and we have set a deadline of July 5th" (eight days before opening night).

The conclusion of Harry's letter to Alec is a poignant plea for understanding: "We know your reasons for the thoughts expressed in your letter, and are sure you understand the problems we have faced and are facing. Extra managerial personnel are being pressed into service on this, and we have full confidence that it will be effective according to the above. I am aware that your future hangs heavily in balance over the outcome of the Festival. May I also refer to quite a number of others who have seriously jeopardized their own positions, and are still doing so, in the common cause. Let us hope that in a short time this evil crisis may be recollected with a smile." Evil crisis! More like *endless* crises!

On the first day of rehearsal in the somewhat less than commodious barn, the only potential problem that we could see was with Irene Worth's contract. Guinness had spoken with her, but she was still unknown to the rest of us. She came, of course, and along with her arrived the only official contract we had with an agent. It was one of the usual contracts you would expect a film star to have: that she must have a hairdresser every morning; that she would need someone to do her nails; that she must have transportation to and from the rehearsals, and so on. There was, as you can imagine, absolutely no way that we had the money to provide Miss Worth with transportation to and from rehearsals, let alone provide her with a hairdresser and a manicurist.

I was so concerned about her contract's stipulations that, the first morning of rehearsals, I picked up Irene Worth in my car and drove her to the barn. She was staying in the lovely, old house of a music teacher named Cora Ahrens. There were merely three blocks between Cora's house and the barn in the fairgrounds where the rehearsals were taking place. Miss Worth climbed into my car, saying, "Oh, this is very kind of you!"

We started chatting, and, about half-way to the barn, she turned to me and said, "I do hope that you're not doing this for me just because it is written in my contract that I have to have transportation."

"Well, as a matter of fact, I must admit it. Yes."

"Oh, don't worry about *that*!" she laughed. "It's just all this agent junk. But I would love to have a bicycle, if I could!"

"Great!" I smiled.

But we had no money for even a bicycle!

My next move was to go to the local bicycle shop, knowing full well that by this time – early June 1953 – the Stratford board was getting pretty edgy about money being spent. So, although I had no authority to do so, I bought a used bike and took it to the office. There was a young lad there named Nester Mitto, who wanted to get into theatre in one way or another. He had just joined us; today, he is a sometime producer in Hollywood.

I asked the fellow, "Would you ride this bike up to Irene Worth's?" But as soon as he left, I was filled with foreboding. "Oh my God! I've given this woman a *used bike*, instead of the promised transportation to and from rehearsals!"

I changed my mind. (A man's prerogative.) I leaped up,

ran to my car, and drove toward where Worth was staying, catching the young man before he got there, and ordered him to bring the bike back. We took it back to the bicycle shop, where, throwing all caution to the wind, I bought a *new* bike for our female star.

The lad then took the bike up to Irene Worth. She was delighted, and she ended up using it all the time. And that was how the great actress ended up with her own, excellent mode of transportation to and from rehearsals – in spite of her agent's insistence otherwise.

Irene Worth was not the only company member who rode around on a bicycle that summer. Stratfordians were already accustomed to seeing Tony Guthrie peddling to and from rehearsals and the theatre site. One day, when the weather was extremely hot and humid, and a thunderstorm threatened to break at any moment, Guthrie quite shocked the locals. Being a very practical man, Guthrie had put on only a very skimpy swimsuit, over which he wore a see-through raincoat. This six-foot-four, apparently nude bicycler was a sight which was, to say the least, not one that was common on the streets of Stratford.

As May turned into June, the news of the Stratford Shakespearean Festival continued to spread. It was written up, as always, in Herbert Whittaker's column in *The Globe and Mail*. ("Most of the world seems concerned with getting Elizabeth crowned Queen of England. Here in this green and pleasant spot, this other Stratford by this other Avon, most of the population is also concerned with the launching of the Shakespearean Festival. For today rehearsals began" – June 2, 1953.)

But it was also discussed in the Windsor *Star* ("Stratford's Move Into Shakespeare Brings City Fame" – June 8), the *Montreal Star* ("Shakespeare Theatre Auditorium Is Almost Ready" – June 17); *The New York Times* ("Canada Pays Homage to the Bard" – May 17); even as far away as the San Diego, California *Evening Tribune* ("A Shakespeare summer season, opening July 13 at Avon, a small city located 100 miles from [Toronto]" – May 27).

Now, if only the good citizens of California could find the Canadian town of "Avon" on a map of Ontario, we would be in great shape!

Meanwhile, back in Stratford, local support continued to grow, as was proven by a rather fascinating, informal "poll" taken that June, reported in *The Beacon-Herald*, under the heading, "MILKMAN CONDUCTS OWN PRIVATE POLL OF SHAKES-PEAREAN FESTIVAL OPINIONS." The brief story is worth quoting in full, because it had ramifications far beyond the pollster's original intentions.

Although Dr. Gallup might not concede the scientific validity of his choice of persons to be interviewed, a Stratford milkman, who has been conducting his own private poll during the last month, is convinced that this city supports the Shakespearean Festival.

Selecting only a few customers each day, the milkman kept a card record of their opinions of the project. At the end of a month, he and his wife spent a Sunday collating and tabulating the results. These were: Local people polled, 304; farmers, 11; foreigners (meaning people from outside the district), 7. Of this number, 258 were in favor of the Festival and hoped for its success; 33 were indifferent; nine were on the fence (these, the milkman claims, were farmers exercising their normal caution); and 22 were opposed.

Questions most frequently asked of the pollster were "How much will this cost?" "What will they do with the tent in the wintertime?" "Will they present nothing but Shakespeare every year?"

(According to Festival officials, the tent will be taken down and stored in the winter. Next year there may be plays other than Shakespeare.)

Those opposing the Festival based their attitude mostly on the cost of the venture. The supporters, many of them people who have never seen a professional Shakespearean performance, were looking forward to seeing the plays with an attitude that could best be described as curiosity.

"I talked a few of the doubters around to supporting it," the milkman confessed, admitting that perhaps he was not as coldly objective as Dr. Gallup would wish.

Well, as you may have guessed by now, the milkman-pollster in question was *my* milkman, Norm Freeman. He would collect money each week on Saturday morning, after he had done his deliveries. I hardly knew him, as he brought his produce very early in the morning.

I was utterly fascinated when he reported his findings to me a few days before he shared them with the newspaper. And I was interested to discover that he had been an usher at the local movie house, the Avon, as a lad.

"Norm, we'll need some ushers for the Festival," I told him. "Would you like to look after handling them?"

"Sure!" he exclaimed.

So that entire first season, Norm Freeman, after covering his milk route at six each morning, came to the theatre and organized local high-school kids as ushers until midnight. Then he would get up the next morning before dawn and resume his profession.

I was aware that this man, who made his living by doing a lot of walking, was afflicted with bad feet. So, later, when actor Douglas Campbell and I decided to start a repertory company, the Canadian Players, I made a proposition to him.

"It'll be a big chance for you, Norm, but I need your help. We're starting an off-season acting company, and I'd like you to be company manager. Discuss it with your wife and get back to me."

The following day, my milkman told me, "When I told my wife about the prospective job, she said that if I *didn't* accept it, she'd divorce me."

And so, Norm Freeman, once milkman and pollster ordinaire, then usher extraordinaire, became manager fair, travelling all over North America with the Canadian Players. On top of this, he was house manager of the Stratford Festival until 1975. All this resulted from one rather innocent, unprofessional, but utterly disarming poll of locals, farmers, and "foreigners" in the early summer of 1953.

12

The Stratford Adventure

During the six weeks of rehearsal, an interesting side-show was taking place. Its origins went back to the famous series of newsreels, produced by the National Film Board, which were a common sight in our movie theatres during and after the Second World War. Older Canadians will recall them well. The series was called *Canada Carries On*, and each newsreel was usually filled with patriotic fervor about our war effort.

The NFB had learned that the Festival tent was the largest of its kind in the world, and they decided that the raising of the tent would make good footage for their newsreel series. So, in June, they sent a three-person crew down to Stratford to film a three- or four-minute piece.

The director, Gudrun Parker, was in our city for less than two days before she got completely wrapped up in the Festival. She soon realized that this was much more than the raising of a giant tent (and an American-made one, at that); this was a major cultural event in Canadian history.

She called the NFB in Ottawa, told them how incredible the project was, and convinced them that they had to cancel other productions they were working on at the time and come up with more money for a much longer film at the Festival. (*We* should have had such luck with finances!)

Two days later, Gudrun's husband, Morten Parker, arrived to film this longer piece. As Gudrun knew more about the Festival from her short visit than anyone else in the NFB, she was assigned the script-writing duties.

Within a week, Stratford looked like a Hollywood set. There were giant trucks, lights, cameras everywhere. The people of Stratford were absolutely stunned by all the attention! The hustle and bustle seemed to say "It's *really* happening here!" Meanwhile, the two Parkers holed up in separate rooms at the Windsor Hotel. Gudrun wrote all night long for the following day's shooting. Each morning, Morton Parker and I waited downstairs in the lobby of the hotel, anxious for her to bring down that day's script. It was that immediate.

Gudrun Parker also sat in on rehearsals, taking note of Guthrie's directions. This is where the problems began. It was clear that Guinness had to be in the film, but the Film Board lacked the money to pay the actor anything remotely close to his film salary.

The business manager of the NFB film unit, Ian McNeil, came to me, filled with concern.

"How are we going to get Guinness in this thing?" he asked me, as we stood in front of the rehearsal hall in the Stratford fairgrounds.

I quickly arranged a meeting between the two of them, during which I stood back and let them talk. I recall Ian saying, "Mr. Guinness, we are making this film, and it would not be complete were you not in it. But obviously we don't have the money that you usually would receive for a film!"

"Well," said the great actor, with a smile on his lips. "I'm sorry, but by contractual arrangement, I cannot accept less than the equivalent of sixty thousand pounds."

At the mention of that astronomical sum, Ian McNeil gulped and said, "Uhh, we weren't thinking so much of a fee, but an honorarium."

"It doesn't matter what you call it," declared Guinness. "It's sixty thousand pounds."

The conversation continued along this line for quite some time, and Ian was getting more and more nervous, although he was still being very nice about the whole thing.

Finally, Guinness offered, "Maybe there's a way around this. By my contract, I *am* allowed to do small, promotional things in films. Maybe we could call this promotional. Do you think so?"

"Oh, you're wonderful!" exclaimed McNeil.

"And about that honourarium you were going to pay me – I think that it should go to the Festival," said Guinness.

Although it was a generous thought, it actually created a real problem, because the National Film Board cannot make a grant to a theatre; but we got around it. So this is why, in the film *The Stratford Adventure*, Guinness plays only himself, since under the terms of his contract, he could not play another character, Shakespearean or otherwise. Douglas Rain, Guinness's understudy that summer, played the Briton's role in the "on stage" sequences.

The film eventually ran forty-two minutes, somewhat longer than the originally planned three- or four-minute item on the raising of a tent! Columbia Pictures handled the distribution, and promptly insisted that the name be changed. The name that the NFB had given it was *Shakespeare's Other Stratford*, which just was not sexy enough for the American-based distributor.

"There's no way that Shakespeare will sell," the man from Columbia Pictures told me.

"But that's what the film is about!" I tried to explain. "We've just had this successful Festival. . . ."

"It doesn't matter. Shakespeare won't sell."

So we changed the title to *The Stratford Adventure*.

I did not mind the name change. I was so thrilled with the fact that it was made at all. It clearly proved national recognition of our endeavours. It is difficult to realize what this meant back in 1953. Today, everyone knows and accepts the Stratford Festival as a Canadian Fact of Life, like the Arctic, or the Trans-Canada Highway. But back then, to have the National Film Board make a major film in (and about) Stratford was unprecedented, and almost unbelievable.

The next interesting anecdote regarding the film occurred when it was being cut and edited, after our first season was over. Around November 1953, I received a call from the director, Morten Parker, expressing concern about the last line of the movie: "And so now, every year, Shakespeare will come back to Stratford."

"Are we safe in saying that?" asked the concerned voice.

"*Yes!*" I bellowed.

The promotional flyer on the film, overflowing with photos

of the performers and even one of yours truly thoughtfully studying the mock-up of the stage, made the film sound as exciting as *Gone With The Wind*.

"THE STRATFORD ADVENTURE!" the folder screams. "A NATIONAL FILM BOARD PRODUCTION. CRITICS ACCLAIM IT! . . . a fine, absorbing, beautifully photographed film – Alex Barris, *The Globe and Mail*. Well-earned applause for a well-made film. . .brilliant color and sparkling narration – Ken Johnson, *Toronto Telegram*. The feel and flavor of an expert documentary. . .one of the most captivating in years – Jack Karr, *Toronto Star*."

And then, on the reverse, what passion, emotion, excitement!

"THE STRATFORD ADVENTURE is the triumphant story of a gamble chanced and won by a Canadian town.

"THE STRATFORD ADVENTURE, filmed in the same true-to-life color as *Royal Journey*, stars the people who first played their parts in real life. THE STRATFORD ADVENTURE shares with you the trials and triumphs, the suspense and joy of an event that made stage history.

"*Come behind-scenes at the Stratford Festival.*
"SEE the patience and friendly good humor of England's Tyrone Guthrie rehearsing a cast of Canadian players.
"WATCH thousands of Stratford citizens as the big top rises over a circular stage modelled from the Elizabethan Globe Theatre.
"FEEL the anticipation and the nervousness of first night with a throng of visitors from near and far.

"See THE STRATFORD ADVENTURE – vital story of a town that became famous for Shakespeare.

THE STRATFORD ADVENTURE
FILM OF A DREAM COME TRUE"

I was quite happy with the final film but I was most charmed by what happened after its *première* at the Avon movie theatre in Stratford in February 1954. As I was leaving the theatre, the now-famous actor Lloyd Bochner, who had come down to view it and who had performed in the first season, walked over to me with a twinkle in his eye and murmured, "Tom, can I sell you a membership in [the Canadian performers' union] ACTRA?"

The film was widely seen. When a number of us from the Stratford Festival went to Russia in 1958, we had a meeting with many theatre folk there. They began asking the then-director Michael Langham about how one operates on an apron stage and other such major artistic questions.

"Look," I broke in. "The Canadian Embassy has a print of a film that was made during the first season, *The Stratford Adventure*, which shows the stage very clearly. If we could screen it for you, then we could talk about it more knowledgeably."

"Oh no," a number of the Russians told me. "We've seen that."

When I was in Washington, D.C., some years after the Festival began, I was staying with the film and drama critic Jay Carmoday, who invited me to a private movie screening. When we walked into the theatre, Carmoday approached the manager to ask if it was all right if I came. The manager came over to me and said, to my complete surprise, "Oh, I want to thank you, Mr. Patterson!"

"For what?" I asked, dumbfounded.

"We've been showing *The Stratford Adventure*, and it's been so popular, that we've had to hold it over the past three features that we've brought in."

The film was even nominated for an Academy Award, which it lost to a Disney film.

As we edged toward opening night, there was endless work for everyone involved, and endless difficulties for Guthrie and the performers. In his autobiography Guthrie wrote about the rehearsals with his usual wit: "The words of the plays are now known, but owing to the acoustics of the shed, no one has yet heard any lines but his own. Lips are seen to move, gigantic but unintelligible noises resound in the building, punctuated by the thumps of baby sparrows hurtling to their doom. These noises make a Wagnerian accompaniment to the *miming* of two Shakespearean plays. It is an interesting new art form; avant-garde but searing to the nerves."

There was also considerable jealousy, as well. People would ask, "Who does Guthrie have drinks with?" Others would say, "Alec came around to my house, and he told me. . . ." There were countless parties, where many Stratfordians vied for the friendship of the major stars. Some people could hardly wait for their parties to finish, so that they could tell others who had come to their house and what he or she said.

I was beginning to feel the serious consequences of my lack of experience. There were a great many details I had to look after, most of which were relatively small, but some, especially financial details, were of utmost importance. I lived in a constant state of worry. Indeed, I was becoming more and more demoralized by what I perceived was a growing lack of confidence in me.

When the Festival had first gained its official status in 1952, I had been appointed general manager. It was a position for which I had no qualifications, and a title which – had I known what it meant (the administration of business) – I am not at all sure I would have accepted.

It did not take very long for me to realize my incompetency in this field. I could not, for the life of me, read a balance sheet or a financial statement, nor did I know about all the details I was required to look after as the "administrator of business." But there was no one else in Stratford at the time who could take the risk of leaving his or her business to start this job.

I did plead with the board to hire a manager, but there was no money to do so. As they turned my request down, they implied, quite rightly, "what are we paying *you* for?"

The board did understand my concern to a certain extent, however, and the suggestion was made that they obtain the services of a retired Stratford bank manager to take over my financial duties. This man, Henry St. George Lee, happened to be a friend of mine. I had gone to school with his children and had had many happy teenage parties in his stately home. But I also realized that this rather patriarchal, conservative former bank official was not the ideal man to control what was then, certainly in the views of many locals, a rather hare-brained scheme which was doomed to failure.

In spite of Lee's knowledge of money matters, I felt that he would be even less "successful" than I was at the position. Fortunately, this plan to approach Lee never did materialize, and various members of the board began to take on more and more of the business details – men and women who still had their *own* businesses and factories to run during this period.

During these last frenetic weeks before Opening Night, I was, in fact, on the verge of complete emotional breakdown. I felt pressure from all directions, even from the "helpful" publicity I had been receiving, almost from day one. A particularly awkward example can be found in a very early column of Herbert Whittaker in *The Globe and Mail* (August 2, 1952), under the heading "A GREAT SHAKESPEARE FESTIVAL/ STRATFORD STARTS THE WHEELS." There, in paragraph three, could be found the kind of line which would only serve to build up understandable resentment against me: "We wish Mr. Patterson the very, very best of luck as he sails off to England on his talent hunt. Great things hang in the balance for all of us. It is appropriate that Mr. Patterson, the Stratford boy who is the "onlie begatter" of this Festival as Guthrie is its Moses, should have the fun of star-catching."

"Onlie begatter"? Here it was, June 1953, with stars in town; with rehearsals taking place; with the tent finally going up; with advance ticket sales actually exceeding our expectations; with the press, both national and, in a few cases, even international, becoming ever more interested, and Tom Patterson should still be regarded as the "onlie begatter?"

In May, *Mayfair Magazine* of New York sent a reporter to do a feature story on Tyrone Guthrie and the Festival for their July issue; we were getting the odd mention in *Variety*; the Toronto papers were doing two or three articles a week on the events taking place in this unlikely "theatrical centre" of Stratford, Ontario. All this publicity was very good for the Festival, but it must have been very galling for Stratfordians, and especially board members, who were working so hard, to read my name over and over again in the press. And the bigger and more important the paper or magazine, the more they zeroed in on the "Local Boy Makes Good" angle.

Looking back, I can easily understand how, under such tremendous pressure, an antagonistic attitude would develop. But at the time, it was not only puzzling, but even hurtful.

Indeed, I did not realize just how far this feeling had gone until one day, about three weeks before we opened, a man came up to me on the street in downtown Stratford, and stated, "Hello, Mr. Patterson! My name is Howard LeGrow, your new manager!"

This came as a complete shock to me. I knew nothing of his being hired. But I think that I more or less covered up my astonishment and replied, with as much sweetness as I could muster, "How nice it is to see you."

Howard, short, heavy, with a round, full face and a pleasant, knowing smile, was another gift from Eaton's, where he had managed the famous Eaton Auditorium. (He had also worked with Jack Arthur at the Canadian National Exhibition Grandstand Shows). He was a godsend, and we remained friends until his untimely death a few years ago. Over the decades, we often laughed at the secret way he had been hired, and how amazed he was that I had actually welcomed him on his first day.

Thank heavens I did welcome him, because without Howard LeGrow, the organization of opening night, from ticket sales to crowd control, would never have gone as smoothly as it did.

But opening night was yet to come: what of those hectic, almost hysterical weeks which led up to it? The only way that tent would get up in time was by arranging a twenty-four-hours-a-day schedule of work, and that is precisely what we did. The chairman called a meeting of all the departments: the building contractor, the plumber, the electrical engineer, Cecil Clarke, Tony Guthrie, and, of course, the genius tent master, Skip Manley. They agreed that, from ten every morning until ten every evening, the theatre would be available for rehearsal. This meant, of course, that all construction had to be suspended during the day. All the building now had to take place during the night.

Pressures continued to build. After each rehearsal in the converted barn, many of the performers would come down to the tent site, to watch the giant canvas go up. It was obvious to me, looking at their faces, that they were very worried whether it would be up in time – regardless of Harry Showalter's heartfelt promises to Alec Guinness.

The most heartening development during those last few weeks before opening night was the camaraderie which grew between such very diverse people. There was Cecil Clarke, who had a very meticulous, almost militaristic mind; Hans Buscher, chairman of the building committee and representative of the Stratford board, who forever watched costs; Bob Fairfield, the architect, who leaned toward the "artistic side" and tended to listen more closely to the Clarkes and Guthries than to the "practical" people; Oliver Gaffney, the contractor, who was more used to building bridges and roads than theatres; Tanya Moiseiwitsch, a designer who was always making surprisingly practical decisions; the Gentle Giant himself, Tyrone Guthrie, who was always good for radical, but, strangely enough, simple, practical ideas; and the plumbers, electricians, and the rest. Despite their differing attitudes and temperaments, this group became so cohesive that it was utterly marvellous to watch them work together.

For instance, the contractor and his men, far from throwing up their hands at the suggestion that they adjust their work schedules around the rehearsals, were quite willing to do so. I was doubly impressed by the artistic people's ability to appreciate the difficulties the contractor had in, say, getting a drain in. If there were any arguments – and there were a number, to be sure – they were usually caused by Buscher, who always felt that he could find some material at a cheaper price. But overall, the United Nations could have learned much had they watched the building of the theatre and the raising of the tent in Stratford, Ontario, in June and July 1953.

It seemed that almost every day presented a new problem to be solved. A group of wood polishers was brought in to finish the stage surface. They gave the stage such a high gloss that it made the performers look as if they were the Ice Capades performing Shakespeare, but lacking the skates. A much-needed night was lost while the gloss so carefully applied was sanded down.

Then there was the strange acoustic peculiarity of the tent, which magnified every sound within miles. Even ball games taking place hundreds of yards away sounded as if they were being played in the front rows of the theatre. Then there were the visitors who spied on the performers during those few weeks when rehearsals took place on the new stage.

In his autobiography, Tony Guthrie commented wittily, and poetically, on that extraordinary period leading up to Opening Night:

For the first few days after we moved into the tent, the rehearsals, particularly in the evening, were an object of great local curiosity.

Multitudes would lurk in the spring twilight outside the skirts of the great tent. On the whole their behavior was impeccable. Occasionally, they would lift the skirts and peek; but only surreptitiously, only occasionally. They knew they must not interrupt. But it was the acoustics which made all this so tricky. A juvenile head would appear under the canvas, momentarily, slyly, six inches from the ground. Then an enormously magnified whisper from outside would say, "WELL?" The head would withdraw. Then the huge whisper would reverberate, "YOU'RE SURE IT WAS ALEC GUINNESS?" The head would reappear. The actors, led by Guinness, would make desperate efforts to get on with the job. Pay no attention. Go ahead. Over the dialogue would float the enormous pervasive whisper: "WELL, WHAT'S HE LIKE?"

Then there were the electric storms. Hardly had we raised our tabernacle before God saw fit to send them – a mighty, rushing wind which made the ropes creak and strain, the canvas flap; the whole great edifice was like a ship at sea, like a film set for *Moby Dick*. Then, bingo! The lightning flashed, the thunder crashed and the rain would beat like a million kettledrums on our roof. She stood it all magnificently; she hardly leaked at all. But great canvas tumours would hang down, where water had collected, diseased-looking, ominous. In the drumming darkness, the actors, rehearsal suspended, would see Skip Manley dash hither and yon, with a knife attached to a long long pole, slashing the tumours. There would be a flash of rubies and diamonds, a ripping sound, and then cascades of warmish, dirty water. Then the sun would burst out and rehearsals would begin again in clouds of steam. It was like preparing a play in a Turkish bath.

The storms passed. But, till half an hour before the public assembled for the opening night, a tiny figure might be seen clambering about on the enormous sagging expanse of terra-cotta-colored canvas; rubies and diamonds flashed in the sunlight, and in the moonlight too, drawing together with exquisite, tiny surgical stitches the wounds he had himself inflicted to save her from destruction.

I soon learned that Skip had a ritual. Before he set up any tent, he bought a straw hat, and would not take it off until the tent was eventually brought down, after the season. He kept the huge needles in the hat, using it as a pin cushion, yanking one out whenever he needed to repair the tent. One of the prize momentos I received from that first season was Skip's hat, which I eventually donated to the Stratford Archives, where it sits to this day, the needles still intact. I sensed that the Oral Roberts Crusades and the Chataquas were just jobs to Skip Manley – he was *part* of the Stratford Festival.

As I recall, there were at least five tornadoes in the vicinity of Stratford during the two weeks before we opened the first season. The closest one came within fifteen miles of the city, uprooting trees, blowing down barns, and cutting off roads. After one of the storms, while the sky was still extremely dark in Stratford, I saw Lloyd Bochner outside the tent watching the clouds. Suddenly the sun came out. The actor came over to me and said, "God is with us, Tom. God is with us."

But because of all the tornadoes, the insurance man, Tom Orr, son of the founder of Stratford's parks system, was very worried what might happen to the tent. He was shopping around for a company to cover us, and was having difficulty lining one up. He and Skip took a trip in Orr's car, circling Stratford, while Skip measured the heights above sea-level in the surrounding area. The tent master returned to Stratford and predicted, "No tornado will ever come within five miles of the city of Stratford."

This assured Tom Orr, who went ahead and landed an insurance company. And Skip has not once been proven wrong in the thirty-five years since.

13

Opening Night

The day of the Opening Night of the first season of the Stratford Shakespearean Festival is one that, frankly, I can hardly remember. I felt a combination of excitement, satisfaction, trepidation, some paranoia, and profound fatigue. Because of the tenseness of the occasion, everybody thought that his or her job was the most important of all. And, looking back on it, this is probably why the big night was such a huge success. From the cleaning staff to the ushers to the box office people, right up to the board members and the artists, each thought and acted as if it all depended on him or her.

On July 11, 12, and 13, dozens of newspapers across Canada carried the same story (compliments of Canadian Press) about the event which was about to take place that Monday: "Hit or miss, theatrical history on an international scale will be made here tonight when a midsummer night's dream, conjured up years ago on the inviting banks of the Avon River, becomes a $250,000 reality."

Even more important in the minds of many – since, as has been often pointed out, Canada has traditionally searched beyond its borders to the voices of others, in order to see if it is *really* successful – the world press was also filled with welcome. "A FESTIVE STRATFORD (ONT.) AWAITS ITS BIG CHANCE TO RIDE THE SHAKESPEAREAN BAND WAGON" wrote Brooks Atkinson in his important "At the Theatre" column in *The New York Times*, on the afternoon of the opening. "The City Hall is decorated with 'Welcome' banners," he went on. "The main street is arched with festive decorations. Arrangements have been made to accommodate about 1,000 visitors in hotels, motels and tourist and private homes." The wittiest headline was above an editorial in The Kingston *Whig-Standard*, in its word-playing reference to the daring thrust stage of Guthrie and Moiseiwitsch: "NO CURTAIN GOING UP".

The coolest heads of all, as I recall, were Tony's and Tanya's, but certainly not the board's. The crowds kept pouring in all day long. Ticket-holders had begun to arrive the Saturday before, and the problems involved just in feeding them had long been apparent. Here was a town of less than twenty thousand souls, with two hotels, neither with more than fifty rooms apiece to rent. They each had their own dining room, but they were built to look after that many people and no more. As well, there were only two other restaurants in all of Stratford that rose above the level of the handful of greasy-spoons and glorified hot-dog stands. We tried to greet as many of the "important dignitaries" as we could, knowing full well that they could never be totally satisfied with their accommodations, and worrying constantly that this might turn them against the Festival.

We realized that with all these men and women pouring into our small city, no matter how good the shows would be, if they could not be fed, it would be *that* which they would talk about when they left town!

So we had a gigantic party before the first performance, taking over the armoury and throwing a dinner for five- or six-hundred people. The armoury was within walking distance of the theatre, which was all the better, as it meant we had a grand procession of men and women in fancy outfits and gowns walking up River Drive from the buffet to the opening night! That buffet settled at least one concern – alcohol – quite well. The restaurants were not allowed to serve any alcohol, but we had a banquet permit to do so that night. (Alec Guinness makes hilarious fun of our province's rather archaic, if not bizarre liquor laws, in his autobiography: "We were rather surprised that in Ontario we had to register at the local liquor store as alcoholics.")

The letter mailed to all the members of the Stratford Shakespearean Festival of Canada Foundation on July 10 is a masterpiece of organization and disarming, small-town concerns:

Dear Fellow-Members:

We are looking forward to welcoming you at the buffet supper in the Officers' Mess at the Armoury before the opening performance next Monday. As we are expecting quite a large number of interesting people, we ask the co-operation of our Stratford members to make the party a success. Will you therefore please note the following points.

1. Please enter the Armoury by the main (Waterloo St.) door, as the wash-room just inside the Albert St. door is reserved for the ladies; the men's wash-room is in the basement. Please register yourself and your guests in the Mess Visitor's book, when you come in.

2. We shall look for you as soon as possible after 5:30. On account of the numbers we should begin serving supper about 6 o'clock, to avoid being unduly rushed later.

3. Supper will be laid out in the billiard room. Please do not linger there after you have collected your food. The lay-out of the rooms is not ideal, and we shall have to keep moving.

4. Please help us to see that our out-of-town guests are looked after.

5. We should begin to move to the theatre by 7:30, going via Parkview Drive. There will be a lot of cars to be parked in a short time, and we must all be in the theatre before 8:15.

6. (This is rather important.) The cost of the supper for those out-of-town guests who have been invited by the Foundation is being covered by certain special contributions – not out of the general funds of the Festival. The charge for Stratford members and our personal guests is $3.00 per person. Mr. Norman Ladd is the treasurer for this party. Will you please pay him before or after the party – not during proceedings, unless you can do it quite unobtrusively.

These opening-night banquets were to grow, over the years. By the second season at Stratford, the town still had no more restaurants and the cost of entertaining so many visitors had become considerably more expensive. Vic Polley, who had then become the general manager and was in charge of the budget, recommended very strongly that we charge the guests, even at the risk of losing some people. He need not have feared. It had become the fashionable thing to do, and the demand was greater than ever. Within a couple of years, the price went up to, as I recall, twelve dollars. We charged this amount, not to make more money, but to try to limit the crowds.

There were, of course, the occasional *faux pas* over the years, some of the most memorable kind. A few years later, after Vincent Massey had resigned as Governor General, he entered the armoury and walked over to the VIP table, where royalty and such were normally seated, and where he had gone in the past. The waiter behind the table came up to Massey and proclaimed, "I'm sorry, sir! This is only for VIPs. You'll have to go over there!"

So Vincent Massey, so recently the representative of the Queen in Canada, picked up his plate and went over to stand in line with the rest of *hoi polloi*!

I have other warm memories of that opening night and the exciting days just before. When Brooks Atkinson, then surely the dean of North America's theatre critics, first landed in Stratford, he checked into the Windsor Hotel. Everyone knew who he was, so they gave him the royal treatment, following which the desk clerk phoned me and announced, "Brooks Atkinson has just arrived!"

It was Sunday, the day before opening night, so I phoned him at the hotel.

"May I drive you around and show you the city?" I asked him.

"I'd be delighted!" Atkinson exclaimed.

I picked him up at the hotel, and we went off to see the Shakespearean Gardens, and then along River Drive, until we finally reached the tent.

As usual, all hell was breaking loose. There was a rehearsal going on; "Slim" Griffith, a local and wealthy industrialist and the husband of one of the board members, was planting trees and flowers; the tent master, Skip Manley, was racing about; and dozens of other people were standing around, gawking.

I turned to Atkinson. "Would you like to go in and have a look at the theatre?"

"No," he replied. "I'm sorry, but a theatre is not a theatre until there's a play in it. I'll see it for the first time tomorrow night."

I was amazed, absolutely amazed, at how well everything went in those few, hectic days, and I still am today, over a third of a century later. The Festival had attracted over seventeen hundred people who poured into our small town. Imagine over two hundred thousand people suddenly descending upon a city of three million, such as Montreal or Toronto, and you have a sense of how busy the town was. All the arrangements were being handled (and handled well) by men and women, most of whom had never been in a theatre, much less any experience of organizing a major cultural event. Since then, whenever I have seen how details have been goofed up on other theatrical occasions, even when run by people who have gone through such organizing dozens of times, I am reminded again of how well Stratfordians handled it all: the box office, accommodations, food, and looking after the press and their often-monstrous egos.

These were reporters and critics from around the world! Prior to that summer in 1953, whenever a reporter from a Toronto paper came to Stratford to cover an incident, it had been a big deal for our town. And now, almost in a trice, we had the press of the Western world there, and the Stratfordians handled it normally, casually, and efficiently.

We took it all for granted, in fact. We had adopted this attitude right at the beginning in the approach we had taken toward "outsiders": Visitors were Festival guests, and we would treat them like guests in our own homes.

There was another important aspect to all this calmness. The local people who had come to work for us had become caught up in the general excitement, and they felt very much a part of the Festival. Their work was not just a job to them; far from it. It was a matter of civic pride, and they wanted all these thousands of visitors to know that we were all friendly people in this little city, and we would look after our Festival guests.

The same attitude was true for the men and women who ran the box office. They were not starving performers, hoping that someone would discover them standing over the mimeograph machine; their job was to run the box office, and they wanted to make it run as efficiently as possible. By chance, that year the CNR shops were starting to reduce operations, and their work-force was being cut down. So, many jobs such as that of stage-door keeper were taken by fellows who had just been laid off from the steam-repair shop, which had once made Stratford thrive (and which had once been the largest of its kind in North America).

To pound out tons of steel one day, and go on to be Host to the World the next, must have been quite a shock to them. But they all handled it beautifully, even the night watchman. Stratfordians and visitors alike were so stunned by the success of the first season that they would come back and just wander around the tent, long after the play was over. The watchman would invite them inside and give them a tour of the theatre, often as late as three in the morning. He had worked in the CNR shops, and he was so proud of *his* new Festival theatre, he just had to show it off.

Another way that the town was involved was shown after one of the first opening nights; I forget which. Brooks Atkinson had written his piece and was out wandering the city the next morning. Right next to the Windsor Hotel was the Fire Hall, where, in the ancient tradition of small-town fire halls, a number of men were sitting around outside, shooting the breeze.

Atkinson drifted up and began to chat with them, since he was an inquisitive man and probably was pleased that they did not know who he was. A fireman on the front steps looked up at the man standing there and asked, "You here for the Festival?"

"Yes," answered the drama critic of *The New York Times*.

"How'd you like it?"

Atkinson rattled off a paraphrase of several paragraphs from the review he had just written along the lines of "I have certain questions about this production. I liked this performer and that one, but I didn't think that the following was very good."

The fireman looked at him sternly and exclaimed, "Listen! Don't you criticize our Festival! Because we have only the best here in Stratford!"

Brooks Atkinson was much amused, and published the conversation a few days later in his paper. He was a theatre critic, not a commentator on the local scene, yet he metamorphosed into the latter, because he wanted so much for this Festival to be successful. It is worth mentioning again that, for many months before we opened, our publicist, Mary Jolliffe, had written to Atkinson regularly, keeping him informed of Festival preparations. So when the critic came to the Festival for the first time, he already felt part of it, because he had known since the previous winter about all the problems we had been having.

Walter Kerr was also there, as were the critics of the other four newspapers of New York at the time. There were reporters, as well, from *Variety*, *The National Geographic*, *Reader's Digest*, *Life Magazine*, *Time*, papers from Chicago, from London, England, even from Vienna. Few of them had even heard of a town called Stratford, Ontario, before that summer.

There had been opposition in the press, of course, right until the last moment. I recall that *The Beacon-Herald* ran an editorial before the opening, headed "AN UNHAPPY CHOICE OF PLAY," which concluded with the thought, "Frankly, this column regrets that a deplorable chapter in history – one which is better forgotten at any time – is being made the centre place of a supposedly 'cultural' crusade. That this hideous blot on Royalty should be featured so brazenly in this Coronation Year of 1953 seems incredibly poor judgment." (To be fair, despite editorial criticism, the town's newspaper was a major supporter and, over the years, has donated a great amount of money to the Festival.)

≶

In spite of all the excitement of opening night, and all that we had worked for, for so long, I was flooded, that big day, with thoughts of the terrible jealousies that still existed on the board. In my mind, I defended my concentration on the press and on publicity, recalling that much of the board had been somewhat anti-press. How could I be blamed for speaking to them so much? I had been a writer with Maclean-Hunter, so I knew how to talk to reporters and enjoyed doing so. But the side effect of my work was that I was now treated as a star by the press. Everywhere the hardworking people of Stratford looked, it was Patterson, Patterson, Patterson, And His Dream Of The Festival, no matter how much I hated seeing it in print.

On the afternoon of Opening Night, when I should have been rejoicing, I thought back to when we had turned the sod for the theatre on April 15. Even then, I had already become an all-too-visible symbol of the Stratford Shakespearean Festival. Many people in Stratford had already grown rather sick of reading about me. Just before we were to grab the shovels, Hans Buscher came up to me and said, "Tom, you really should be turning the sod, but I think that it would be better if you didn't." So Harry Showalter did the (dirty) deed. It was at that point that I became fully aware of just how double-edged my reputation had become. I was even being accused that I was only out to get my name in the paper.

But then there was Herbert Whittaker from *The Globe and Mail*, who, the weekend before the curtain did *not* go up, wrote about the significance of the Festival, soothing any wounds that were still open:

> Up to Monday, the description of Stratford, Ont., in the Encyclopedia Britannica, as "a city and port of entry of Ontario, Canada, and capital of Perth County, situated 83 miles W.S.W. of Toronto by the Canadian National Railway, on the Avon River," will still hold. After that date the important information and identification of the town of Stratford must include: "Site of the annual Shakespearean Festival, opened by Tyrone Guthrie, Alec Guinness and the faith of the citizens of Stratford on July 13, 1953."

And in time we think that even the local paper will recognize the glory which has come to this town, transforming it from a C.N.R. convenience into a citadel of poetry and theatrical imagination.

In particular, Stratford's Festival has already achieved a major importance in the theatre of the country. I think I am exact in saying that it represents the first dramatic production in this country which has been conceived on a full financial scale, selecting its talent from the best over a large area, creating its own kind of theatre, calling on internationally respected leaders. After it, we can never sink back, unknowing, into the kind of theatre we have suffered through these pioneer years, trapped into mediocrity by low budgets, exploiting its actors, audiences and even managements.

On Monday a milestone in our theatre will be passed. And, if we may be permitted a prophecy suited to the occasion, we would say we see it as the first great festival in this country, the first of a series by which the national culture may be shaped and explained to match our more materialistic development.

Who was I to argue?

14

The Reviews Come In

On the evening of July 13, 1953, the Stratford Festival presented its first production to the world: *Richard III*. The storms had stopped – at least those outside my tortured mind – and the weather had turned out to be beautiful. The trumpets sounded out Lou Applebaum's original fanfare, followed by the fire of cannons set off by a small contingent from the Perth Regiment. (The reverberations through the tent of the shot caused near heart failure in many of the theatre-goers, who had not expected it.) Carl Stoermer's giant bell rang, the lights dimmed, and Alec Guinness, in his striking Moiseiwitsch costume, his left eye drooping precipitously and memorably, entered on the balcony, giving voice to the brilliant words, "Now is the winter of our discontent. . . ."

I sat in the front row and let the realization that the Festival was actually taking place, that we had, incredibly, managed to pull it off somehow, sink slowly in. The tension and worry I had been living with for so long slowly dissipated, and I was overcome by fatigue. I was so very tired, I was not able to appreciate the play. Fortunately, because of all the action, the many battle scenes, and the actors declaiming within three feet of where I was sitting, it was nearly impossible to fall asleep. Although, I must confess, my eyelids drooped several times during that very special evening. (I was startled wide-awake when a noise, which was to plague most of the season, roared through the theatre – the whistle of a passing train.)

I do remember very clearly one line which haunted me. When Richard is planning to get rid of his first wife (played by Amelia Hall), he tells some of his minions, "Rumour it abroad that Anne my wife is sick and like to die." It hit home, because so many of those involved with the Festival would have loved to do the same to me. That line, which I heard every second night, constantly reminded me of how many were after my neck, even after the Festival had opened.

The evening went perfectly, and when the play was over, there was a long, standing ovation, which seemed to go on forever and was interrupted only when Alec Guinness came out alone, still in costume. He made a brief speech, "I want to pay tribute to the only man who could make this possible – William Shakespeare," at which point the applause began again.

Large numbers of people rushed up to me, tossing off such lines as "Remember at the beginning, when you told me about this idea? I just *knew* it would work!" (Not bloody likely, as Liza Doolittle might say.) Indeed, perhaps the most honest person who approached me that evening was John Bassett, the publisher of the Toronto *Telegram*, whom I had approached for money in the early stages of the planning and had turned me down. "Jesus Christ, Patterson!" he blared. "I thought you were the stupidest sonovabitch who ever came into my office! And you proved me wrong! It was a great evening!"

Here is a sampling of the most interesting, the most critical, the most important press reviews of *Richard III*:

Lauretta Thistle, music and drama editor of the Ottawa *Citizen* wrote:

> With a brilliant fanfare of trumpets, a salute of cannon and the breaking out of a flag, Stratford's first annual Shakespearean Festival opened last evening, and the performance of *Richard III* was as stirring as the sound of the trumpets.
>
> The emotions of the crowd of more than 1,400 as they

filed into the circular tent-covered theater may have been a mixture of hope, fears, chauvinism and curiosity. But when they came out all their thoughts were for the excellence and the genuine excitement of the production. . . .

Guthrie uses masses of people. His kings are attended by whole groups of pages. When he stages a battle, the theater is full of sound and movement. Banners and shields and crosses are more than life size.

The costumes are voluminous and vastly colorful and they serve at times as scenery as well on the unadorned wood which comprises Tanya Moiseiwitsch's new style stage.

Morley Safer (who would go on to fame and success on the television programme "Sixty Minutes") wrote in the Woodstock, Ontario, *Daily Sentinel*:

On the first Elizabethan stage ever used in a large scale production, since the days of Queen Elizabeth herself, Alec Guinness, top flight British star of stage and movies unwound the tale of Richard III last night. Mr. Guinness was accompanied by an equally competent cast made up mainly of talented Canadians. . . .

William Hawkins wrote in the *New York World-Telegram and Sun*:

Canada's Shakespearean festival opened with a history-making explosion last night by a production of *Richard III* that is nothing less than brilliant.

Alec Guinness, playing the title role, and Tyrone Guthrie, directing, offered a production of the bloody, violent play with novel depths and excitement I rarely have had anywhere before. . . .

This Richard is far and away the finest thing Mr. Guinness has been seen in on this side of the Atlantic.

For Mr. Guthrie it is a great triumph. He uses this remarkable new stage with admirable fluidity. The action comes from before and behind the audience. It comes up ramps and down aisles. The stage is a permanent set platform and stairs, changed rarely and slightly.

Mr. Guthrie uses all these levels and direction for magical pageantry with black guards, tan soldiers, white-robed choir boys and colorfully garbed councilmen. In the final battle scenes, the play takes on such violence that the audience last night was dodging as none ever did at the most startling 3-D movie.

Herbert Whittaker in *The Globe and Mail*:

The most exciting night in the history of the Canadian theatre has ended here with the final curtain [!] on Tyrone Guthrie's production of Richard III at the opening of the five-week Stratford Shakespearean Festival. . . .

A memorable production and a memorable night in the theatre for Stratford and Canada. The final word of praise must go to the people of this festival town, and to Tom Patterson's dream, a dream come violently and excitingly to life.

Walter Kerr in the *New York Tribune*:

The whole improbable adventure got under way last evening with a generally robust performance of *Richard III*, and it's a tourist-trade natural on several counts: A superb light comedian gets a crack at the bloodiest villain of them all and a Shakespeare chronicle is turned into the speedy and spectacular rough-and-tumble it was meant to be.

Mr. Guinness is fun to watch. Maybe too much fun. He begins the evening by strolling out into a projecting balcony and swinging one leg over its side like a slightly dour monkey. He rolls his tongue in his cheek with a devastating relish, weeps crocodile tears with garish abandon, and brings confident craftiness to his ghoulish romance with the freshly widowed Lady Anne. . . .

But Mr. Guinness has played so much of the evening so lightly that he has prepared neither himself nor us for

the open torments of the dawn soliloquy, or the final
agonies of defeat. The performance is always interesting;
but it still falls short of this monster's full stature. . . .

Tanya Moiseiwitsch's costumes are everywhere breath-
taking, and Louis Applebaum's incidental music is steadily
helpful. Especially interesting in the supporting company
are Robert Christie as Buckingham; Edward Holmes as
King Edward; Douglas Rain as Tyrrel, and Eric House in
several brief roles.

The full roar of Shakespeare's *Richard* may be missing
from this summer-time excursion, but Stratford it still in
possession of a jaunty, colorful show.

And finally – although there were dozens more, including the
ubiquitously reprinted review of Canadian Press – here is the
complete review Brooks Atkinson wrote for the *New York
Times*:

Spectacular production; shallow performance. That may
be the quick way to describe the *Richard III* that opened
the Shakespeare Festival last evening, with Alec Guinness
as the deformed, dissembling Duke of Gloucester.

Tyrone Guthrie, director, and Tanya Moiseiwitsch,
designer, who recently collaborated on the Old Vic *Henry
VIII* for the Coronation, have now created an original show
out of an ingenious setting, stunning costumes and fluid
movement.

The stage in Stratford's inviting tent theatre is a variation
on the Elizabethan open platform. A thin apron projects
deep into the auditorium. A formalized setting of wooden
columns and stairways provides several acting levels; two
entrances from the cellerage add another dimension to the
performance and make for continuous variety in Shakespearean showmanship.

Miss Moiseiwitsch's costumes are bold and beautiful.
The designs are powerful, the materials are rich; the
contrast in color and shape is dramatic. When Mr. Guthrie
sets the actors, costumes and props in motion, summoning
state processionals from the pit or setting opposing armies
at each other's throats on the various stage levels, this

is a *Richard III* that looks exciting. Every detail has been meticulously planned and the spectacle is imposing.

But Shakespeare's bloody drama of evil and consequence comes off at second best amid such overpowering externals. As the scheming Duke of Gloucester, Mr. Guinness does settle down to work in the last act, when he plays a king hedged about with treachery and forced to fight for his life. Richard, bitter and beady-eyed on the throne; Richard, brooding on the prospects of battle; Richard, coldly crossing swords with Richmond – these are Mr. Guinness's finest scenes and the most coherent moments in the entire performance.

By the time of the third act, however, it is almost too late to make a headlong melodrama out of the legend of the evil genius of the House of York. For Mr. Guinness is a brilliant comedian, and he plays the first two acts in a light, witty key of subtle persiflage.

He omits the malignancy of a notoriously revolting character. On these terms his performance is frequently amusing, but at the expense of Shakespeare's character and drama. For it is difficult to believe that any of the nobles or church and state officers of medieval England could be won over by the frivolous Richard that Mr. Guinness describes in the first two acts.

As old Queen Margaret, Irene Worth gives a penetrating performance of real quality. Her acting has scope and bravura in the style of one of the furies. And Robert Goodier's resolute, cool-headed Richmond helps enormously to put into balance the dramatic forces of the last act. Both Miss Worth and Mr. Goodier also respect the literary qualities of the writing. Without formalizing the verse, they give it the distinction of rhetorical speech.

Although Robert Christie's Buckingham has voice and stature, it conveys little of the cynical opportunism of that forceful man of mind and action. The cast is a long one, but generally competent and talented, for Mr. Guinness is better supported than many stars who play Shakespeare.

No doubt the company, in time, will develop a team spirit that will produce uniformity of style. At present, the acting does not get much beyond the surface of this wild and horrifying play. The performance lacks the rude, elementary, concentrated power of an Elizabethan acting piece.

Mr. Guthrie and Miss Moiseiwitsch are chiefly responsible for that. They have concentrated on production. Infatuated with the mechanics of a very original stage and the ominous spectacle of a historical chronicle, they have left the drama loose and superficial. Amid all the furor of his melodrama, Shakespeare did have a theme – cold-blooded evil and hot-blooded consequences.

Alec Guinness's own recollection echoes that of Atkinson, interestingly enough. In his autobiography he notes, "we knew the Festival had got off to an emotional and blazing start (in spite of my poor Richard)."

Poor Richard or inspired Richard, when the play came to its violent conclusion that opening night, my emotions matched it. It was an electrifying night for everyone. I heard someone say that if the Russians had wanted to put Canada out of commission, all they had to do was bomb the Stratford Festival that evening, because almost everybody who was anybody in Canada was there.

Part of the excitement came from the experience of being in a tent theatre. Many people had come with the expectation of finding a tent thrown up in a field somewhere. So when they saw this massive canvas in all its colour and majesty, it was as if we could have put on anything, and they would have been satisfied.

Because of all the excitement, and because there was another opening the next night, Cecil Clarke had announced that "there will be nobody allowed backstage after the performance." I took him at his word, and although I was one of the last to leave the theatre and wanted to go backstage to congratulate the performers, I stayed away.

Alas, Guinness was furious when no one showed up. He thought "they haven't even come back to say thank you, let alone what they thought of it!" There was hell to pay later, until we were able to explain to the performers our misunderstanding. But that first night, the actors were left alone, with strict orders not to party until after the second opening, Tuesday night. Imagine – after a thrilling opening in a revolutionary new theatre, there was no celebration.

Less than twenty-four hours later, we would all be watching a very different production of a very different play – one that, according to Tony, had not been performed professionally for over two-hundred years – Shakespeare's *All's Well That Ends Well*. Which, as we quickly discovered, was exactly the right epithet for the inaugural season of the Stratford Shakespearean Festival.

15

Another Op'ning, Another Show

With all the electric excitement that greeted our first opening night, and with all the accompanying obligations (dealing with the press, worrying about the dinners, handling the Big Shots who were pouring into our small town), I'm afraid that I remember very little about the opening night of *All's Well That Ends Well*.

It was a beautiful show, and the excitement which followed its conclusion was even greater than the night before. The press was almost uniformly ecstatic, and the audience was in a state of euphoria. I had never seen Canadians so excited, and would not see anything like it again until the opening of the Montreal festivities of Expo 67, celebrating our country's centennial, over a dozen years later.

But to me, the most exciting thing was getting a telephone call the next morning from Brooks Atkinson.

"Mr. Patterson?" said the gentlemanly voice.

"Yes?" I replied, still groggy from the night before.

"I thought I should tell you first, because as far as I'm concerned, last night Guthrie pulled a play out of the ash can, and set it on a pinnacle. Can we have dinner?"

Now, major critics – even minor critics – do not normally call up so-called producers, but this one certainly did. And it established a tradition, which lasted until he retired. On the day following each opening night, Brooks Atkinson and Tom Patterson would go out to lunch or dinner. (Although it would be several years before Stratford had any first-class restaurants, it must be admitted.)

That first summer we were joined for dinner by Atkinson's wife and their grandson. His wife was a great antique collector, who spent her time in Stratford browsing in our little stores as she did not care for Shakespeare much.

"I'm sorry that I couldn't be very kind to *Richard III*," Atkinson apologized.

"Oh, that's okay," I answered. "That's what you're here for."

"Maybe if I saw it again," the critic offered, "I might have some second thoughts for my Sunday piece."

When I heard that there was going to be a piece in the Sunday *New York Times*, which has such a massive readership around the world, I eagerly agreed.

As with so many aspects of that first season, we had no idea whatsoever how besieged we would be by the press – and so we never had enough tickets for them set aside. Whenever some reporter/critic would come in without notice, he or she never thought there would be any trouble to get seats in this "country festival."

When Mary Joliffe had run out of her allotment, she would quickly rush to the office staff – Florence Pelton and Fran Tompkins, who had recently been joined by Vera Banks – and together, they would dig into their respective purses and gather the money to buy the tickets from the box office. They figured that, later on, they could somehow get this money back. (And they were right.)

Then, Mary would report back to the latecoming critic, in a most professional way, "You can pick up your tickets at the Box Office tonight!"

This kind of co-operation and enthusiasm went on throughout that entire first summer. It mattered not what crisis arose, these people, Pelton, Banks, and Tompkins – later joined by Fran Lightbourne, the Archdeacon's daughter, and several others – would inevitably rise to the occasion in both orthodox and unorthodox manners.

When I tried to get tickets for Brooks, I took him and his grandson down to the box office. As usual, there was a riot of people, struggling and begging to get tickets. I knew that I couldn't get through there, so we went around to the stage door, worked our way past performers putting on their make-up, and made our way through the auditorium.

"I'd like two tickets for tonight's performance of *Richard*," I requested of the house manager.

"Have you seen the mob out there?" he replied.

In other words, there were not two tickets to be had. As if this were not clear enough, he added, "If I show my face out there in the box office to ask for favours, I'll be killed!"

"There are no more tickets, Brooks," I said to him and his grandchild, as we walked toward the exit. "I'm terribly sorry."

"I couldn't be more pleased" he replied, referring to the obvious success of the Festival.

Suddenly, the house manager reappeared.

"I can give you two seats in an area behind the tent poles, where the line of sight is poor."

So Brooks Atkinson and his grandson sat three-quarters of the way back, behind these massive Douglas Fir poles, leaning around them to watch *Richard III*. And he wrote a Sunday piece, which appeared on the front page of *The New York Times* Entertainment Section that weekend, which raved about this new Festival up in Stratford, Ontario.

Thanks to the inspired network set up by Mary Joliffe, the reviews went out by wire, which meant that the telegraph operators could track us down and give us a sense of the reviews even before they hit the papers (on the line of "He loves it"; "He thinks it's so-so.")

Three years later, in 1956, the Festival produced *The Merry Wives of Windsor*, a comedy in the same vein as *All's Well That Ends Well*. Brooks Atkinson simply hated the production, but then, two seasons later, in 1958, a magnificent production of *Much Ado About Nothing* came along, which Brooks adored. It starred Eileen Herlie, among others, and it was, indeed, a superb evening of theatre.

However, whether from faulty memory or his sheer enthusiasm for the new show, Brooks wrote "This is the best thing Stratford has done since *The Merry Wives of Windsor*."

When Atkinson was sending this copy over the wire, the telegrapher noticed the mistake, but, of course, had no legal right to make any change. So he immediately phoned Mary Joliffe, and reported the error, adding that "I'm sure that Brooks will want to know, otherwise he will be so embarrassed!"

Fortunately, this was just before I was about to partake in my annual luncheon ritual with the theatre critic. I knew that his opening comments to me would be, as always, what he thought of the show. I had every expectation of hearing him tell, in conversational tones, what he had just finished writing and sending to New York by wire.

Sure enough, when we met in the lobby of the hotel in Stratford, Brooks' first line to me was, "I loved last night, Tom. It must be the best thing you've done since *The Merry Wives*."

I had my opening. Very innocently, I looked at him and said, "Don't you mean *All's Well*, Brooks?"

Up to this time, Brooks had always been a very quiet, soft-spoken gentleman, who never seemed to show any excitement. But at the realization of his mistake, he practically ran back to his room, and got on the phone to the telegraph operator, and then *The New York Times*. I had never before seen him in such an agitated state!

As fate, fortune, and men's eyes would have it, Brooks caught the error in time, and was saved from making this possibly foolish mistake. And it was all thanks to the Stratford telegrapher, who had somehow remembered – better than the great theatre critic – what Brooks Atkinson had written several years before!

There was a party after the second opening night, financed by my mother, believe it or not, at the cost of about seven hundred dollars. This was a goodly sum, in those days. My salary for the first twelve months of the Stratford Festival, which did not start pouring into my bank account – and quickly out – until January 1, 1953, amounted to only $6,000. So I was delighted that my mother was able to host the party, not only for the people who had done so much to make the Festival happen, but also for the many (several hundred) important visitors, who by their attendance gave their stamp of approval to the project.

It was a fantastic party. Not only were the cast and local Festival supporters there, but also the literati of Canada, as well as politicians, business leaders, theatrical celebrities, and *la crème de la crème* of the North American theatrical newspaper world. Of the latter, many, even in the short period that we had known them, became good friends of publicist Mary Jolliffe and myself. They became even greater supporters of the Festival because of the camaraderie that was established by this party.

But, as important as this celebration was, it was only one of many that were to take place that year. Because the Festival was so exciting and so new to the Canadian psyche, each night seemed like Opening Night to those who attended. They all wanted to celebrate, even into the sixth week. For those of us on "the receiving line," it was, or seemed to be, one long party. The guests, whether they were press, or VIPs, or just interested supporters, were on holiday and exhilarated by the excitement of participating in a new and world-class project.

Today, it is hard to imagine how we had to share our time one evening in the Golden Bamboo restaurant between hosting Jose Ferrer and Rosemary Clooney (on their honeymoon) and an influential judge from New York, when they were sitting at tables across from each other, each party vying for our attention!

This kind of partying went on for the whole six weeks, almost every night. Rightly or wrongly, I thought it my job to attend as many as I could. I do not deny that I loved it, but occasionally I found it tedious. And there was the inevitable criticism from some Stratfordians that "All Tom wants to do is party." After the performances and the inevitable parties, I used to get home very late. And I mean very, very late.

In spite of their experience of hosting this international theatre crowd, Stratfordians still insisted on stolid small-town conservative manners. So, for the first two or three weeks after opening night, I felt obliged to walk on the lawns and jump over the sidewalks, so that I would not wake the neighbours, and create even more gossip than already existed.

Finally, I realized how ridiculous this was, and taking the bull by the horns, I walked, noisily and bravely, down the centre of the pavement. Not only did I feel better, by taking the secrecy out of how late I was getting home, but I also took the "juice" out of the gossip. In other words, when it became *so* obvious that "Tom Patterson has been getting home at 3:30 or 4:00 a.m.!", it was no longer a subject for discussion. Everybody knew!

As the many parties of that first season followed the performances, the following mornings I was often not as alert as I should have been. But, once the season started, the Festival ran smoothly and I was not needed as much. The men and women who staffed the theatre were determined to do a good job, so there were few organizational problems I had to attend to.

Nor were there problems on the critical front. Guthrie's production of *Richard III* was not universally cheered, but his *All's Well That Ends Well* was an undeniable success. Here are some of the more interesting comments from that second Opening Night:

Harvey Taylor in *The Detroit Times*:

All's Well That Ends Well, a sort of heavy-handed compromise between a bedroom farce and a royal court comedy of manners, moved onto the stage of the Stratford Shakespearean Festival last night – a stage which the night before had been drenched with the blood of King Richard's many victims.

Alec Guinness and Irene Worth were again stars and both demonstrated the flexibility and versatility of their styles – Guinness in a polished interpretation in the fairly passing role of an ailing French monarch and Miss Worth with a delightfully graceful feminine treatment of Helena, a scorned bride who sets about to win over her husband with a series of implausible but ingenious stratagems. . . .

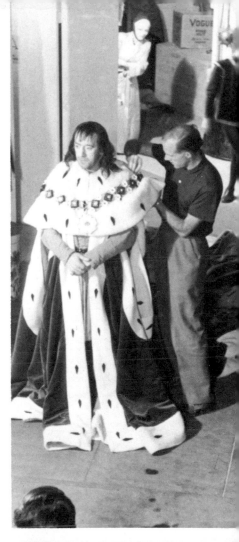

ABOVE LEFT Bob Goodier and
Tyrone Guthrie at the dress parade
for *Richard III*. (*Peter Smith & Co.*)

ABOVE RIGHT Stratfordian Gordon
Jocelyn dresses Alec Guinness as
Richard III. (*Walter Curtin/Public
Archives of Canada/PA-142699*)

RIGHT Vice-president Alf Bell
welcomes Sir Ernest and Lady
MacMillan on opening night. (*NFB/
Public Archives of Canada/PA-156104*)

ABOVE LEFT Richard III (Alec Guinness) woos Lady Anne (Amelia Hall) after he has had her husband slain. Shortly after this scene he uttered the line that scared Patterson: "Rumour it abroad that Anne, my wife, is sick and like to die." (*NFB/Public Archives of Canada/PA-156502*)

LEFT The accepted leader of the company, Douglas Campbell, as Hastings in *Richard III*. (*Peter Smith & Co.*)

ABOVE RIGHT "The day is ours, the bloody dog is dead." The slaying of Richard (Alec Guinness) by Richmond (Robert Goodier) at Bosworth Field. (*Peter Smith & Co.*)

CENTRE RIGHT Bill Needles (*left*) and Eric House (*right*) murder the Duke of Clarence, Lloyd Bochner. (*Peter Smith & Co.*)

BOTTOM RIGHT Toronto *Globe and Mail* drama critic, Herb Whittacker (*left*), Zelda Fitchandler, founder of Arena Stage in Washington, D.C., and John Buist from *The Times* of London, England. (*NFB/Public Archives of Canada/PA-156510*)

ABOVE (INSET) Douglas Campbell as the garrulous Parolles in *All's Well That Ends Well*. New York critic Brooks Atkinson raved about Campbell's performance and declared that Guthrie had "pulled a play out of the ashcan and set it on a pinnacle." (*Peter Smith & Co.*)

ABOVE Irene Worth, Beatrice Lennard, and Amelia Hall in a scene from *All's Well*. (*Peter Smith & Co.*)

LEFT Eric House, Douglas Campbell, Robert Goodier, and Peter Mews in *All's Well*.

RIGHT Alec Guinness and Irene Worth. The bathchair was loaned to the Festival after Herb Whittacker wrote that one was needed in his column in the *Globe and Mail*. (*Peter Smith & Co.*)

ABOVE Vincent Massey meets Alec Guinness and Amelia Hall backstage. (*NFB/Public Archives of Canada/PA-156507*)

LEFT Feigning great interest, Governor General Vincent Massey inspects files during his visit to the Festival offices. Vera Banks (*centre*) and Florence Pelton, when they heard Massey was coming, rushed out and bought these "filing cabinets" to impress him. (*The Beacon-Herald*)

BELOW Three of the Canadian actors who performed during Stratford's first season. *From left to right*, Timothy Findley (*Ken Bell/ Stratford Festival Archives*), Robert Christie (*John Steele/Stratford Festival Archives*), and Don Harron (*Stratford Festival Archives*)

ABOVE Harry Showalter says
goodbye to Judy and Tony Guthrie
and to Tanya Moiseiwitsch as they
leave Stratford shortly after the
opening. (*Peter Smith & Co.*)

RIGHT Jose Ferrer and Rosemary
Clooney visited the Stratford
Festival during their honeymoon.
(*NFB/Public Archives of Canada/
PA-156509*)

TOP Producers Robert Whitehead, Elia Kazan, and Jo Mielziner study plans of the Stratford stage with Tom Patterson. They came to Stratford for design help with the Lincoln Center in New York.

ABOVE LEFT Broadway producers Herman Levin and Billy Rose. Rose distracted the audience during a performance of *Richard III* by following the play in a script on his lap. (*NFB/Public Archives of Canada/PA-156505*)

ABOVE RIGHT In 1977, the Stratford people paid Patterson the great honour of naming the island in the Avon River, the Tom Patterson Island. Here, Mayor Betty McMillan unveils the plaque. (*Stratford Festival Archives*)

As in the opening night's performance, the crowd scenes were handled with excellent timing in a sort of ballet-like precision.

Herbert Whittaker in *The Globe and Mail*:

Tonight, as the festival's second offering, and alternate play to Richard, they gave us another gift and a delightful surprise in their *All's Well That Ends Well*.

One might well extend that remark to say that they gave the world of the theatre a gift, for *All's Well* has truly fallen into discard and is here revived and brought to unsuspected beauty and wit. There is something of Miracle in its rebirth. . . .

In all, I should say that the demands of *All's Well That Ends Well* find the Canadian actors in the company better suited perhaps than for the high ritual and turbulence of *Richard III*. It seems that the performances, although fewer, were more closely successful and original.

John Beaufort, in *The Christian Science Monitor*:

The Stratford company turns from the sanguinary business of *Richard III* to the elegant sophistication of *All's Well* in a performance of lyricism and robust comedy. The costuming suggests both the Edwardian and the contemporary; the feeling is largely romantic. Since the play included a number of Shakespeare's coarser passages and employs a repugnant plot, Mr. Guthrie and company have achieved something remarkable in creating a performance that is gay, beautiful, and disarming. As for Miss Worth, she made a delectable Helena.

Donald Harron's Bertram is not so much the worldling and cynic as he is a blindly headstrong young man determined to live his own life. Although gulled by the ridiculous coward, Parolles, he is not truly infected by the fellow. But his reconciliation with Helena still seems a work rather of contrivance than of natural development.

Mr. Guthrie and his actors have provided a thoroughly charming and imaginative performance, presided over by

Mr. Guinness as a gravely benign and forgiving King of France. As Bertram's mother Miss Stuart plays with a grace and beauty of voice which are a constant joy. Mr. Campbell gets not only the fun of Parolles but for just a moment something more touching in the man's self-revelation.

The production reaches its comic heights in the hilarious interrogation of the blindfolded Parolles by his soldier comrades and its visual heights in the ballroom proposal scene during which Helena chooses Bertram.

It is a lovely production in every way.

The Stratford festival has begun auspiciously.

And, as he had hinted to me that Wednesday morning when he had invited me to join him for dinner, Brooks Atkinson rhapsodized in his July 16 review in *The New York Times*:

After enjoying the Tyrone Guthrie production of *All's Well That Ends Well* in the Stratford Festival tent theatre last evening, one can easily understand why Mr. Guthrie and Alex [sic] Guinness have selected this minor comedy to alternate with *Richard III*.

In what amounts to modern dress, *All's Well That Ends Well* is like an elegant ballet that discloses the accomplishments of an excellent acting company. It would be impossible to find in North America another company so finished in comedy style and so attractive personally.

All's Well That Ends Well provides a congenial setting for these players, not that it is any great shakes as a play. A minor Shakespearean potboiler, it is so excessively minor that it seldom gets on the stage. Derived at second hand from a Boccaccio anecdote, it has an artificial and rather distasteful plot.

It insists on regarding a heel as hero and, especially in the first act, it abounds in the sort of word fencing that may have seemed brilliant in Shakespeare's time but seems puzzling today. To practically all of us, *All's Well That Ends Well* is a new experience in the theatre because hardly anyone regards it as worth putting on the stage.

No doubt Mr. Guthrie, as director, concedes all that in

advance. For the first half-hour you may still be wondering why he selected it for a Shakespearean festival. But then the director's design for the performance begins to emerge through the prolixity of the text; and *All's Well That Ends Well*, providing the validity of its title, grows increasingly fascinating throughout the evening.

The modern dress is no affectation. In period it is not contemporary or fashionable but just modern enough to take Shakespeare out of the distant past. The costumes are stunning: they are imaginatively designed and conspicuously well made. Although Tanya Moiseiwitsch's formalized setting seemed almost too self-conscious for *Richard III*, in which the actors hardly had room enough to play, it suits *All's Well That Ends Well*, and, again, the lighting is ingenious.

Mr. Guthrie's performance flows without effort across the apron stage up and down the stairs through the forest of columns and out of the ports in the pit. It is a spontaneous and delightful bit of inventive theatre in good taste and good humor.

As the King of France who, as a matter of fact, is a secondary character in the play, Mr. Guinness is in his top form. Bearded and bewigged into an aging monarch, he plays with grace and command, like a man so used to authority that he does not have to mix arrogance with it. As the unhappy wife who has to spend the evening pursuing a sullen husband, Irene Worth gives another superb performance that overflows with loveliness, devotion, ceremony and modest guile.

In the part of Parolles, the swaggering soldier and blustering buffoon, Douglas Campbell gave an enormously funny performance in a broad style of clowning and pantomime.

In fact, all the actors bestow excellent character portraits on this production. Eleanor Stuart's fine-textured performance of a lady of quality who is amiable and reserved at the same time; Michael Bates' old counsellor who has considerable gusto behind the courtliness of his manners; Donald Harron's handsome, priggish, high spirited young husband; Beatrice Lennard's enchanting Diana with a mind of her own; Amelia Halls' raffish and blowzy widow of Florence, these are distinguished pieces of work.

As the director, Mr. Guthrie has made much ado out of practically nothing. He has squeezed all the fun out of an old fable without losing his sense of style and a sense of daintiness in the acting.

It seemed as if everyone was happy, even the performers. And how could they not be? The Stratford board had decided, three days before opening night (moved by Mr. Kaye, seconded by Mr. Crone), that "gifts be bought for Mr. Guinness and Miss Worth; a book be bought for Dr. Guthrie and a bag for Mr. Clarke." Let it never be said that we failed to be generous, right from day one!

There were the occasional problems during that first season, as might be expected. Our worst problem continued to be the extraordinary amplification of outside noise in the tent. The minutes of the July 24 meeting of the board read: "Mr. Patterson was asked to see if anything could be done to stop the noise from the ball games and Dr. Showalter to see what can be done to lessen the general noise."

We had a fight on our hands, from both the future Mickey Mantles and the present Nightly Trains. When we approached the ball teams and begged them to hush up during performances, their response was, "Hell, we were here before *you*!"

This was undeniable, even if somewhat Philistinic. And we could have done without their rejoinder: "*You* make a lot of noise in there with those cannons going off, too!" (We argued uselessly over whether cannons affect a ballplayer's concentration as profoundly as cries of "Slide!" and "You're out!" affect a performer's.)

It was not until the second year of the Festival that Vic Polley secured a solution. Vic was an athlete who had played on these teams, and he struck a deal with the ballplayers that, if there were any empty seats, he would invite as many as possible to see the show for free, as long as they agreed to stop playing by eight-thirty each night. And thus, a new phrase entered baseball vocabulary around the globe in the mid-1950s: "Game Called On Account of Culture."

To be fair to the ballplayers, that first summer they did not foresee that the Festival would become an annual event. But by the second year, the importance of the Festival to the community was fully realized, and the problem was easily resolved.

The "general noise" referred to in those board minutes was really quite serious, although its resolution was almost comical. A train went through the town of Stratford, Ontario, at 8:35 every night. Evidence of this disconcerting noise was captured in the NFB film, *The Stratford Adventure*, in the scene in which Tyrone Guthrie stops a rehearsal to allow a rather noisy train to go by, across Ontario Street, barely three blocks from the Festival tent.

During the whole of the first season, the train whistle blew at 8:35 each night. We could have set our watches to it, if we had wished to do so. (Many would have preferred to listen to Alec Guinness, Irene Worth, and the others on stage.)

Then, at one point during the Festival's second year, Donald Gordon paid the Festival a visit. Gordon was the president of Canadian National, which, amongst other things, owned that infuriating train. I still remember him sitting in the front row of the theatre, watching and listening intently to the production unfolding before him, when the whistle blew. Seventeen hundred pairs of eyes turned to stare down at him. The huge man sank slowly into his seat.

Within a week, the schedule of the CN train through the town of Stratford, Ontario was miraculously changed. From that day on, the train raced through the city limits at 8:25, just five minutes before the plays began. Of such coincidences are great moments made.

Noise was not the only problem that the tent-theatre gave us that summer. Another was the dreadful heat. Temperatures during performances sometimes rose as high as 110°F, and almost every night the local St. John's ambulance had to assist someone who had fainted.

Many suggestions were made for air-conditioning systems, but none were practical for our tent. Eventually, Frank Wilkins, a Stratford ice man (they were still delivering blocks for ice boxes in those days) came up with a homespun solution. At his suggestion, we built a two-storey shack on to the back of the tent. The floor boards that separated the two storeys were laid two inches apart from each other. Wilkins stuffed burlap into each of these two-inch gaps in such a manner that the burlap hung in curtains throughout the lower floor. A huge fan was procured, which blew a strong wind through these curtains. For the rest of the season, Wilkins filled the top storey each day with fresh ice, which, as it melted, soaked the burlap curtains. The fan blew the icy air from the hut, through the backstage, up through the tunnels that led to the stage, and into the auditorium.

This innovative air-conditioning worked, more or less, for the audience, but the actors, who had to make their entrances from the cold, damp tunnels, complained mightily.

For a final authoritative pronouncement on our tent, which I heard that summer, I give you Billy Rose. "The best tent theatre in North America," proclaimed the owner of the Diamond Horseshoe, originator of the "Aquacade," and producer of many Broadway musicals. "Any tent-theatre we have in the United States can't touch it," he said. "Your sight lines are better, your design is better, and your acoustics are better. That coco-matting was a good idea."

Billy Rose had lunch with Tony Guthrie and his wife, and then returned to the big city, but not before declaring that "a lot of New York actors and actresses are eager to play Shakespeare."

"Are you planning to do such a production?" he was asked by a *Beacon-Herald* reporter.

"No," he replied, firmly.

16

Unsuddenly, That Summer

Brooks Atkinson wrote, too kindly, in his Sunday *New York Times* article on the Festival, "If Mr. Patterson is feeling considerably relieved this morning, theatre-goers everywhere are going to feel grateful to him for the next month during which the festival continues. For the Stratford Festival in Ontario is a genuine contribution to Shakespeare in North America."

And so, I hope, it has proven to be. But during the summer of 1953, the events were still rushing upon me – and the myriad of others who were responsible for the Festival's success – too quickly for me to really appreciate the accomplishment.

The concerts were one example. Early on, we had decided that the Stratford Shakespearean Festival should also provide musical concerts for the theatre-goers who would be pouring into town. Louis Applebaum had been retained by Tyrone Guthrie as composer for the incidental music for the plays and for the fanfare which still heralds each performance. He also conducted the orchestra after the Festival opened. But at the same time, although no one knew it, he had contacted Walter Homburger – at that time a young agent in Toronto – to become the "impresario" for some concerts to take place in the Festival tent.

Applebaum and Homburger, with practically no time at all to organize, miraculously came up with sixteen afternoon concerts featuring such budding stars as Glenn Gould, Jan

Rubes, Lois Marshall, Gerhard Kander, Albert Pratz, Ed McCurdy, John Knight, and James Milligan.

Soon, cards circulated throughout the city announcing: "STRATFORD SHAKESPEAREAN FESTIVAL CONCERTS PRESENT: CANADA'S OUTSTANDING ARTISTS IN ONE-HOUR CONCERTS IN THE FESTIVAL THEATRE. JULY 21 TO AUGUST 14, AT 4:15." The admission, you may be shaken to read, was exactly one dollar per person.

Mainly because of the difficulty in publicizing these concerts outside the town in the short time between their arrangement and presentation, the audiences were very small. It seems all but impossible to believe now, but when Glenn Gould played his first concert in the tent, Governor General Vincent Massey, along with his staff and a few Festival board members – about a dozen people – formed exactly half of the audience.

Tony Guthrie's job was essentially finished when the two plays opened on July 13 and 14, and when he left a few weeks later, there was little fanfare. The cast got together, went to his wife, Judy, and asked what they should get him as a present.

"An award set up in his name," she quickly replied.

So they approached Tony and asked him if he would accept it.

"Yes," he said, "but only if there are no rules and regulations. It's to help Canadian theatre, so I don't care if the money is to pay the doctor's bills for a good actor." In other words, Tony did not want the award merely to pay for a year at a school, unless the performer wanted that.

The cast raised money by collecting donations and organized with the Festival The Tyrone Guthrie Benefit Award Performance.

They have done this for thirty-four years now, and have set up a committee to accept applications from men and women, as well as recommendations from others. The award can be for theatre management, dancing, singing, hairdressing – anything. In 1986, the award was $10,000, and was given to several theatre people. And 1987 will mark the thirty-fifth year of the Award being given to worthy workers at Stratford.

On the final night of the season, we organized a party which was a complete disaster. We had planned this party for the cast and a few others in a downtown location, but the performers wanted their own party at the theatre before they left, for which they dreamed up a number of different sketches and skits – parodies on Shakespeare and things of that sort.

Alec Guinness decided not to go to the party at the theatre. Instead, he went home after the final performance to get dressed for the later party. I spent the evening with a friend, and had planned to attend the downtown party later. At about one in the morning I started walking toward the party through streets that were strangely empty and silent. I could see only one other person in the distance, who turned out to be Guinness.

"What has been going on?" I asked him.

"The party was supposed to start at twelve-thirty," Alec told me, "but there's nobody there, and the doors are all locked!"

So Alec and I walked up and down the street, waiting for others to show up. What had happened was simple: The skits were going on endlessly at the Festival Theatre.

Finally, the other performers began to arrive, and the downtown party started to swing. By this time, Guinness was pretty fed up, and he had good reason to be. Ottawa's famous curmudgeon of a mayor, Charlotte Whitton, was present, as was the fine actress Amelia Hall, who was an Ottawa girl. As bad luck would have it, the party was soon usurped by the Ottawa contingent.

It was as if Mayor Whitton had never before had such an audience, and she rapidly took over. She gave Hall a fur coat and countless other presents. Everyone else just stood there embarrassed and upset, including Amelia Hall. The party was supposed to be a closing night celebration at the end of a quite remarkable summer in Canadian cultural history, and Whitton turned it into a tribute to Amelia Hall, alone. In brief, to quote from Nathan Cohen's famous description about Richard Burton's version of *Hamlet* many years later, the party was "an unmitigated disaster."

After the closing party fiasco, I had what can only be described as a nervous breakdown. I had lived through over a year of nearly non-stop tension, excitement, disappointment, and ecstasy; a year-long, emotional roller coaster. I went home and found my wife crying, also from sheer fatigue. Our second son had been born just three weeks before the Festival opened, only adding to our sleeplessness and tension. I began to curse every man, woman, and their brother to the point that I finally called the doctor and told him that he had to come over and help me.

My wife quickly calmed down once she saw how hysterical I was. When the doctor, Gib Jarret, an ardent Festival supporter and a humorous, gentle man arrived, he practically had to hold me down. He finally gave me a shot to knock me out.

As it happened, Alec Guinness was to leave the next day, and I was not well enough to say goodbye to him. To make things worse, he was still angry about the dreadful party of the night before.

My wife phoned Alec on my behalf.

"Tom's in a bad state, Alec," she told him. "Could you come down to see him?"

Alec refused, not knowing just how bad off I was.

"But Tom wants to say goodbye to you," she went on. "Can we come down to the station to see you off?"

So my wife wrapped me up in blankets and took me down to the train station which had provided so many memorable 8:35 p.m. noises over the previous few months. I must have looked like hell warmed over, for Alec finally realized how sick I was, and that I was just as upset as he was about the conclusion of the season. We parted, at last, on quite good terms.

Mixed in with the emotions that were breaking me down was my distress at not having enough money to provide properly for my growing family. My wife phoned Hume Cronyn and Lloyd Bochner to tell them how ill I was, and, luckily, the two of them truly understood my pain. Hume came around to our house and shook my hand. When I looked inside it, there was a $500 bill rolled up. It was a low-point in my life, but receiving such a generous gift was about the nicest thing that could have happened to me at that time.

Literally as well as emotionally, everything seemed to come apart. The tent was struck almost immediately. The balcony and pillars were all removed, as well as the countless seats, the stage, dressing rooms, and lighting equipment. The blue canvas "ceiling" and the blue and red exterior tent, which weighed over two tons, were unlaced and the sections placed in giant bags for storage. Part of the theatre's concrete shell was boarded in and used as storage space for some of the props.

The place that had overflowed with men, women, and Shakespeare for the previous few weeks now looked like a wasteland. It symbolized my emotional state.

My mind was flooded with thoughts and memories: the heat within the tent, which had led to many people fainting over the course of the summer; the tornadoes – possibly as many as eight or ten, and the largest number ever to hit the area – which had swirled around the town but had never hit the centre of Stratford itself; the heavy thunderstorms, which had forced us to stop some performances while the rain drummed loudly on the canvas roof.

The dismantling of the tent brought to mind one more, quite extraordinary fact, and one which has never been related before now. The pressure for tickets had been so overwhelming, throughout the season we kept adding seats. We were able to do this because the auditorium was surrounded by a movable inner tent hung within the major one. So although we started with 1,780 seats, we actually ended the season with over two thousand. It will never be known just how many there were. But I know this much: We announced that we were playing to 98 per cent houses, because we did not think that anyone would believe us if we said 100 per cent. In truth, our fine actors had performed before over-full houses, as we were accommodating far more than our original seating capacity.

As if the breaking up of the magical combination of tent, personalities, and summer – as well as my total exhaustion –

were not enough, I was now required to give a speech at the Canadian National Exhibition. Long before, I had accepted the CNE's invitation to talk about the Festival to an audience that would include the gifted Victor Borge, who was performing at the Ex that week. There was only one week to go, and I was in no shape to answer a telephone, much less give a major talk.

It was then that one of the quiet heroes of the entire Stratford adventure came through for me – in addition to Lloyd Bochner, who was providing considerable moral support. Floyd Chalmers of Maclean Hunter invited me to his home in Toronto, and told me, "I've got a backyard that's fenced in. There will be no press. Nobody will know where you are. You can just rest and get back into shape."

Which, thanks to Floyd, is exactly what I did. I was able to write and to deliver that speech. Because it flowed so directly from that extraordinary first summer of the Stratford Festival, I think that it is worth quoting in its entirety:

I speak to you today as a Canadian – one of those peculiar in-betweens; neither British nor American; one of that race known as the tillers of the soil, the hewers of wood, and the miners of vast natural resources.

And yet, in recent years, we have become something different, something broader. And over the last four months, Canada has become known in the newspapers of the world for something else, something almost foreign to our way of life, something – let's blurt the word right out – something Cultural: one of the greatest theatrical successes of all time.

The build-up to Stratford has taken much longer than that. We, as Canadians, have been preparing ourselves for our new cultural role ever since the War. We would not admit that we were becoming interested in it, but that is what has been happening.

The first time I really realized this was in my first letter to Tyrone Guthrie, who directed our plays at Stratford. In attempting to outline the Canadian scene to him, one of the things I pointed out was that Canada had, up to the present, been too busy getting its bread and butter to worry about any dessert. Now we had probably too much bread and butter and were not certain what we wanted to round out the meal. But then I listed all the things that we were attempting in order to make a slightly more satisfying feast. There was the unprecedented growth of Little Theatre groups; professional theatre groups; the Royal Conservatory Opera Company, doing such fine work with its Festivals; the Lois Marshalls and Betty Jean Hagens; the growing love and knowledge of ballet; our Jack Arthur, whom a few years ago people accepted sceptically when he took over the Grandstand show; the increased consciousness of Canadian painting and sculpture; the high place our radio drama was taking in international competition; the National Film Board; our proudly Canadian writers.

And after I had finished this letter, I read it over and decided that we really have nothing to be ashamed of. Our record since the war has been good.

And so the Stratford Shakespearean Festival came. Naturally we went through many soul-searching sessions. The small committee of Stratford businessmen often wondered what they had got themselves into.

We were told that nobody would come from Toronto to Stratford, a distance of 100 miles, to see Shakespeare. Where are you going to put the people? was another question asked. And, believe it or not, sometimes these were asked in almost the same breath. I often felt that there must be a combined answer to these two problems but could never quite figure out what it could be!

In spite of enormous difficulties, Stratford was a huge success. And I think it is not too early to try to study that success. What did it do for the actor? What did it do for the audience? What did it do for Canada?

For the Canadian actor, the main thing Stratford did was give him a sense of pride. For years, he had been a underling, in some cases treated as almost a parasite in this country of great material producers. At last he had achieved a status, not only in Canada but in international circles, as a "Canadian actor." This was especially important, because this status was achieved not in New York or London, but in Canada. They read from Brooks Atkinson's column in *The New York Times*, "the greatest classical comedy company on the North American continent," and could hardly believe what they saw.

Acclaim came from other New York papers, such as William Hawkins in the *New York World–Telegram and Sun* who called it "the greatest step forward in Shakespearean production that this continent has ever seen." Detroit, Cleveland, San Francisco, Washington, Buffalo, Toledo, and Chicago papers joined in the chorus – and later the London *Times*, the *Manchester Guardian*, and other English reviews trickled in, all very flattering to our Canadian actors.

Almost overnight, and completely unconsciously, the Canadian actor took on a new dignity, and I am very happy to say, a new humility. He had achieved success and yet was in such exalted company that he was made to realize what that success entailed.

Stratford also gave the actor a sense of standard. I would suggest that most of the Canadians in the company are not going to be satisfied with any lessening of that standard. This is going to have its effect on the productions you see in the immediate future. Indeed, it already is apparent in the enthusiastic and difficult programme which the Jupiter Theatre has set for itself here in Toronto. And the rumors of other major ventures in Canadian theatre.

But what of the audiences – these people who would not come from Toronto to Stratford to see Shakespeare? Well, they came from Toronto and also from New York; Hawaii; Greenland; Los Angeles; Miami; Hollywood; Rome, Italy; Victoria, B.C.; from London, England, and Medicine Hat, Alberta. They came from South America and Kapuskasing; from every state in the U.S.A. and every province in Canada.

It is, of course, difficult to say what any experience has done to any audience – and I think some local incidents will do more to illustrate what Stratford did for Canadian audiences than anything else could.

The Festival had its effect on citizens of Stratford long before the actual productions started. One small bridge club of four women started to read *Richard III*. They ended up as a nine-week study group in Shakespeare with 150 members.

If anyone had asked a member of the audience why he or she was there, one would have got a wide variety of answers. Many came, of course, because they realized that here was something big; something they had never seen before. Many came to see Alec Guinness; others because they thought they should support a worthy project, or because it was the thing to do socially. But what most of them came for was simply to see Shakespeare.

This was no high-brow or arty crowd. Shakespeare himself would have been happy to see what a representative cross-section of people he was attracting. Here was the real Shakespearean audience of the Elizabethan day – the ironmongers of the CNR shops, the craftsmen from the furniture factories, the butchers, the bakers, the seamstresses, all standing in line with the patrons of the arts.

There was one other section of the audience which deserves special mention. It is an audience to which the "Ex" has a special appeal: the school children and teenagers. Naturally, most of these were Stratfordites, but many also came from great distances. These children, who had been brought up on a diet of what I like to call "examination Shakespeare," were the most enthusiastic and most responsive part of the audience. Many in Stratford have seen the shows six or eight times. Don't try telling those kids that Shakespeare is uninteresting or dull!

Why, up there now, the kids no longer play Buck Rogers or Space Cadet; they play Richard and Richmond with wooden sticks as swords.

The wider reaction of the Festival is just as surprising – what did it do for Canada? Well, Sir Shuldham Redfern, former secretary to the Governor General and a leader in the Arts Council of Great Britain, wrote in his London Letter to the *Montreal Star*, that the Festival had done more to cement Anglo-Canadian relations than any other single event since the war. In the same vein, James Minifee, in his Washington letter to the *Telegram*, Toronto, said that

Stratford had crowded out official releases from Ottawa on a question which at that time was of important economic consequences. The same reaction came from the press all over the Western world. When, if ever, have papers from England, France, Germany, Yugoslavia, Brazil and the United States concentrated to such an extent on an event in Canada? And for that interest to be concentrated on a cultural event is, I think, unheard of.

And yet this cultural event got greater coverage in the international press than our great discoveries of iron ore and uranium.

So one of the advantages to Canada was in the fact that the Festival not only advertised the country, but it helped in the most difficult problem of our day: international relations.

It worked as well inside the country, too. It gave Canadians a pride in their country. They could hold up their heads amongst visitors as an adult nation. When theatre was mentioned, they could for the first time in the country's history, say, "Oh, yes, the Festival at Stratford," and nobody would laugh.

There is another important angle. When I was first selling the idea of the Festival, I used the story about young Canadians leaving Canada; you know, the thing that is always good for a subject when an editorial writer is short of an idea. I used the story so much that even I got sick of it.

But to my complete amazement, the Festival proved the death of that story, in the theatrical field at least, even before it opened. Don Harron had already booked passage for England when he heard about the Festival. As soon as things showed the slightest chance of becoming reality, he cancelled passage. Why? Because he could get more in Canada of what he wanted than in England. Similarly, the Festival brought back Canadians like Douglas Rain from London's Old Vic. Jonathan White and Jo Hutchins also returned from England. From New York came Lloyd Bochner and Norman Roland.

Some of these people are remaining in Canada because

of the increased activity here. Others are returning to their winter homes, but all are coming back to Canada next year.

The Stratford Festival gave Canada something else, a little more practical perhaps, but important: It gave us another potential export. Up to now we have been exporting the raw material – Mary Pickford, Marie Dressler, Walter Pidgeon, and more recently, Hume Cronyn. Now we have the finished product, which in a year or two may be invited to the Edinburgh Festival, to New York, to Yugoslavia. And it will go to these places as a product completely manufactured in Canada.

But, you might say, "Oh, yes, but there is not enough Canadian talent to keep this up." I disagree. You have undoubtedly read somewhere or other about Canada's "vast, untapped resources." I suggest that one of the main resources we have failed to develop is the latent talent in this country.

And so the Festival is over. It has accomplished a great deal – helped the Canadian actor, given our citizens a sense of pride, advertised Canada in a way nothing else could, even helped international relations.

But what should we expect of future Festivals?

I think it is not insignificant that one of the greatest military leaders of our time, Field Marshall Montgomery, stressed the other day that Canada must develop a Canadian culture. (You know, I used to try to find an alternative for the word "culture" but found nothing suitable. It makes one feel really happy to see it returning to its rightful place in our language.)

"Monty" proved in his speech that a Canadian culture was necessary from a political and military point of view. The fact that the Festival took place at all proves that certain businessmen also hold that point of view. But we do need wider acceptance of the fact – and that is where the Festival can play its biggest part in Canadian life. It can help, by being a focal point where young aspiring artists can reach out to, to develop the culture which is necessary before we can say that we are really mature.

Being an exciting thing, it will interest people as it did this summer. Then those deadly speeches on culture will no longer be necessary. [I was overly-optimistic!]

So that is Stratford's first job – to make artistic endeavour exciting and to help develop a Canadian culture.

The Festival must also prove, as it has done to a certain extent this year, that cultural events can be economically operated. But if they are going to show a profit eventually, they must be done on the highest scale. That is what the public demands. The theatre, just like any other business, needs capital to get started. It needs support over the first few years of its operation. But if it is managed correctly, it can be just as profitable as any other business.

It would not be right to close without paying a special tribute to the small group of English artists who did so much to make Stratford possible. I start off with Tyrone Guthrie, whose productions created a sensation in the theatrical world. Then that completely unselfish and great actor, Alec Guinness, who was so helpful in sharing his knowledge with our Canadian actors. (He had many of them at his home on many occasions, always helping them out with any trouble they had, or making suggestions as to their future.) Cecil Clarke, whose work in the production of the two shows was a little short of incredible; his wife, Jacqueline Cundall, who did more than anyone else to build up a theatrical trade in Canada through her training of young Canadians in property management; Irene Worth, Douglas Campbell, and Michael Bates. Ray Diffen, and his assistant Annette Geber, who cut all the costumes for *Richard III*.

In summing up, I would like to quote part of a letter which Tyrone Guthrie wrote to Alec Guinness last year. He said: "Canada is likely in a few years to be the richest and most powerful country in the world. There is a great sentimental urge in Canada to be influenced by Britain; there is a great practical urge to be influenced by the U.S. Almost every common sense argument, based on geography and economics, drives Canada and U.S. into each other's arms.

"If we, the British, are as tactless, as stupid and as

apathetic about this as we look like being, it's just going to be George III and the Boston tea party all over again.

"We, you and I, have a chance in this project to make an exceedingly conspicuous, and therefore potentially useful gesture in favour of Anglo-Canadian co-operation. I have never before felt so convinced of the obvious practical value of anything I have ever been asked to be connected with."

After hearing that, what Canadian has the effrontery to have an inferiority complex about Canada's place in the world of today?

Thank you.

When I returned to Stratford, I learned that all my files had been put in the garbage, ostensibly because they had to make room for next year's. Still, I found it strange that only my files were dumped, and none others. Fortunately, I had a considerable number of copies at home, so at least part of my record of that year still exists. But a good deal of archival material was lost to the garbagemen.

I still do not know who did it. But ultimately, even the loss of my personal files seemed a petty issue. The Stratford Festival had begun, and it looked as if it would continue.

It has.

17

The Canadian Players

In the months following the excitement and activity of that first summer, the town of Stratford seemed to close up like a cocoon. There was very little to do, and little work going on. As early as the end of August 1953, all the actors had left town and no tourists were coming in. Because the season was so short – unlike today, when the Festival runs up to five months, even more – there was an endless hiatus.

I continued to receive all kinds of invitations to speak, for which I did not charge (at first!). I considered it good advertising for Stratford and its Festival; how could I turn any down? So I was out of town a great deal. But each time I returned, I could still feel the antipathy toward me as the putative father of The Success Story of 1953. As well, I was still suffering from profound fatigue.

By this time everyone – including myself – had come to the realization that this guy Patterson was no general manager. But, as I've tried to make clear, had I been a true general manager in the real sense of the term, there never would have been a Stratford Festival! Any real general manager would have nixed the impossible dream before all that money was spent. Indeed, I feel that this is one of the main reasons why most attempted festivals, of any kind, fail to get off the ground. So-called "practical" festival organizers demand to know – and justifiably so – how much is this thing going to cost? and how much will it make, or lose? We neither had the time, nor the inclination, to puzzle over these questions too long, and we had blundered our way to success.

But because of the lingering resentment against me, it became clear that I had to look to my own future rather than depend upon the Festival for the rest of my life. After all, I was still in my early thirties, and had a growing family to support.

As I pondered my future, I kept thinking about the comment that Tony Guthrie and some of press had made about the lack of theatrical activity in Canada. While many of the Canadian performers at Stratford in that season were good, all of their training had come from CBC radio, where they had worked on such programmes as Andrew Allen's "Stage" series. But speaking into a microphone does not train one for projecting to an auditorium, whether at Stratford or anywhere else.

Furthermore, all chances of the Festival company staying together and going on tour in any foreseeable future had died, because of the high costs of travel. The difficulties we had encountered during that first summer in one place made it clear that one cannot just pick up a company of five-dozen or more actors and actresses and tour across North America. Such tours require a lot of organizing and planning – not to mention money. A major tour was out of the question. But what of a tour on a much smaller scale?

Spurred on by my decision to get off the painful hook of being the Festival's general manager, I convinced myself that, because of the explosion of acclaim that the Stratford Festival had garnered in 1953, it might be possible to take some of the performers from the Stratford company and do a limited tour of small, Ontario towns.

My plan was to take this new company to such towns as Kitchener-Waterloo, Galt and Hespeler (now known as Cambridge), and London – places neither too far away nor too expensive to organize – with the hope that we would eventually grow to the point of taking on a national tour. These limited tours could easily take place during the Festival's long off-season.

I must admit that I was thinking of this touring company as a means of graciously getting out of Stratford because of the build up of tensions. I also knew that the man to lead this company was Dougie Campbell because of his leadership, talent, and pioneering spirit.

I wrote to him in January 1954, and he wrote back exactly what I had hoped: "Yes, Tom. I've been thinking of the same thing. We should do it!"

In 1953, Campbell had left his family back in the Old Country, but when he came back in early May 1954, he brought his wife and two children with him. They took the overnight train from Montreal to Stratford, where I met him at the station. There was Dougie, in his bedroom slippers, just out of his berth, together with his wife and kids (including his son Ben, now in the Stratford Festival company and a great actor).

Alf and Dama Bell had also come to the station to greet the actor. Campbell loaded the family into the Bell's car and announced "I'll go in Tom's car." We both fell to talking about a touring company, much as Tyrone Guthrie and I had burst into discussion of our proposed Stratford Shakespearean Festival, barely two years before. We spoke at a mile a minute and quickly came to the conclusion that it was a very good idea.

As I had expected, there was some opposition to the idea from the Stratford board, who basically wondered "what's Tom up to, now?" But by this time, Dougie had secretly lined up a number of actors for our new company, including Bill Needles, Bruno Gerussi, and William Hutt, all of whom have become, and still are, major forces in this country's theatre scene.

We decided to do Shaw's *Saint Joan* as our first offering, to be cast almost entirely from inside the 1954 Stratford company. We also lined up Norm Freeman, who had had such terrific experience as my milkman and as the head of the Stratford ushers, as company manager.

It was now June 1954. We had to think up a name. As it happened, two of my good friends were in town that week: John Beaufort, the drama critic of the *Christian Science Monitor*, and Sol Jacobson, a leading Broadway press agent.

I invited them over to discuss the subject of our touring company with Campbell and me. I could talk to these fellows a lot easier than to the Stratford board. (After all, to many of them I was still just a local boy; what could *I* know?)

Sol made the all-important (and rather interesting) observation: "There must be 'Canada' in the name. Canada is a standard of quality of theatre, today, because of the Stratford Festival."

In the middle of this discussion, an actor from the company burst into my house, crying, "Dougie! You gotta come now! There's *trouble!*"

Doug rushed out, without even saying goodbye to my rather influential, as well as supportive guests. John Beaufort turned to me, smiling, and declared, "I wish I wasn't such a nice guy, Tom! What a story I could make out of this!"

(And there was quite a story to be made, too. There was terrible tension in the company in 1954 about Cecil Clarke's direction of *Measure For Measure*. The performers were deeply dissatisfied with his *modus operandi* and wanted Tyrone Guthrie to take over from him. Tony, who was busy directing his extraordinary production of *Oedipus Rex*, flatly refused to undercut his long-time friend and assistant, but did, eventually, help out with the direction of the Shakespearean piece.)

Shortly after this unpromising session, Doug and I went before the Stratford board. We had deliberately waited as long as we could to do this because we wanted to present them with a *fait accompli* they could not stop. Then we made the announcement to the press: The creation of Canadian Players, with Douglas Campbell and Tom Patterson as co-founders.

We soon got Lady Eaton interested, and she became our patron. To be blunt, none of this would have come together without her initial support. She gave us a number of contacts, and gave us a very generous $5,000 donation.

A further example of our good fortune involved an "international" involvement. During our first season, a businessman in Detroit named Sol Krim, who owned a movie house which ran art films, had organized a trip by the University of Detroit Players to come up to the Festival and make a presentation of a scroll to Alec Guinness.

When Canadian Players came together, I decided to ask Sol Krim to sponsor us. And lo and behold, he donated $3,000 to our little company. In retrospect – and even then – it was quite amazing that an American movie-house owner would support a Canadian theatrical company. I am pleased to report that we did eventually perform in Detroit.

Campbell, of course, was acting in Stratford's second season, so we could not begin rehearsals for the Canadian Players until the season finished. This coincided with the end of the camping season, and so we rehearsed up at my wife's camp in Haliburton. Dougie directed the company, in which his wife, Ann Casson, played the title role in the Shaw play. The rest of the company of eight had to double and triple their roles. I went to only a handful of rehearsals, as I was mainly occupied with lining up the tour.

Our opening night was hardly as earth-shattering as the one back in July, 1953, on the revolutionary new stage in Stratford, Ontario, but it is still a pleasant memory for me. It was, in fact, absolutely fantastic. It took place in Ottawa, during the first (and only) time that the South East Asian Treaty Organization held its annual meeting in Canada. From my years working on the Stratford Festival I had good connections with the External Affairs Department, and I obtained their sponsorship for the opening night at Ottawa's Little Theatre on October 5, 1954.

Saint Joan was performed in full, but in rehearsal clothes, on a bare stage. The audience that first night could not have been more colourful. Far-Eastern delegates in their native dress were sprinkled about the auditorium, looking far more interesting than the actors on stage. The British High Commissioner was there, howling at all of Bernard Shaw's witty jibes against the English. Meanwhile, the Asians, many of them survivors of British rule, kept looking over at the man to watch just how much he was enjoying it.

We played ten performances in Ottawa, to wildly enthusiastic reviews. But, eventually, the audiences dwindled away to practically nothing. Then, we were off to Smith Falls, Peterborough, Kingston, and other eastern-Ontario towns and cities.

I went to each community in advance of the company and met with the press, since we had little, if any, money for advertising. Theatre was so new to most of these places that the local newspapers were glad to write articles on the Canadian Players. We were booked up until that Christmas; then we took our most memorable tour of that first season.

Our most recent patron was Colonel Reynolds, the head of Ontario Northland Railroad. He had been to Stratford during the 1954 season, and had begun a friendship with Dougie Campbell. We both talked with the Colonel about Canadian Players, and he promptly offered to take us all up to Moosonee, in Northern Ontario, at no cost.

I told a correspondent of *The New York Times*, Tanya Daniels, who had covered Stratford, about this coming adventure, and she joined us to follow the story. I, alas, developed the flu and stayed at home.

Doug Campbell, as I recall, asked Colonel Reynolds, "Is there enough electricity for our lights, up there?"

"Sure," he replied.

"But it *is* a very small town!" insisted the actor.

"That's okay. I'll just request that everyone turn out their lights during your performance."

Which they did.

The posters, which had been made up for the entire tour, had a blank space for the time and place of each performance. At Moosonee, someone had scrawled, "CURTAIN: 8 O'CLOCK, OR ONE HOUR AFTER TRAIN ARRIVAL."

Our performance took place in a Nisson hut in Moosonee. It was jam-packed, mainly with native people. In the parking lot outside were snowmobiles, a ski plane, and even a dog team. Indian children were brought by their parents to sit on the floor in front of the audience, so they could witness our *Joan* on a cold, bare stage, and in rehearsal costume.

Soon after the play began, Tanya Daniels saw a movement outside the window. There, in a huge grey parka, at 40⁰F below, was an Indian scraping frost off the window so that he could watch the performance in the packed hut.

The audience adored the play (the native kids fell in love with Bruno Gerussi), and we got a five-column head in *The*

New York Times's theatre section, together with a picture of the native man staring through the frosty window, unable to get inside to see the play.

Romantic, perhaps, but neither romance nor rave reviews pay wages. We still had no money. So I went down to New York and eventually lined up a performance of *Julius Caesar* with the Canadian Players on the famed "Omnibus" series, which brought a welcome infusion of cash into our company. The TV show received the second highest Nielsen rating of the year, beaten only by a Leonard Bernstein Children's Concert.

The summer after the Canadian Players's first tour, Tony Guthrie returned to Stratford to redirect *Oedipus Rex*. He turned to me one day and said, "Without even being told, Tom, I can sense which performers were in Canadian Players, due to the development shown in their acting skills."

Over the next twelve years, Canadian Players performed productions of *Macbeth*, *Man and Superman*, *Othello*, *Arms and the Man*, *Twelfth Night*, *An Enemy of the People*, *Private Lives*, *Playboy of the Western World*, and *The Importance of Being Earnest*, among others. I, personally, remained with the company for only about a year and a half, and was replaced by my first wife, Robin, and Laurel Crosby.

The Canadian Players ended up visiting and performing in every Canadian province, and all over the United States. We even had an agent in New York, to handle American bookings – a man introduced to us by John Beaufort. As often as possible, performances were sponsored by local women's clubs, the Rotarians, or other community organizations. During the summer seasons, hardly a week went by without a performer being visited in Stratford by someone who had seen – or befriended – him or her in Moose Jaw or Antigonish.

What led to the Canadian Players eventual demise? Or perhaps that should read, what led to its *inevitable* demise? During the period we were touring with actors who earned perhaps $125 a week, television was coming to this country. As actors on television, performers could earn far more, and in the comfort of their own homes, so to speak. It became unfair to ask men and women to traipse across North America for low wages, and, indeed, it eventually became nigh-on impossible to get good performers to do this.

Perhaps I should conclude this brief look at what almost naturally grew out of the Stratford Festival – Canadian Players – by recalling an incident in March or April 1955, when our touring season was winding down, and the Festival was gearing up for its new summer season in the city.

"Tom?" yelled one of the young women in our box office.

"Yes?" I replied.

"Did the Canadian Players just perform in Kapuskasing?"

"Uh-huh. Just last week. Why?"

"I *thought* something must have happened up there," she replied. "Because we just got a flurry of orders for Festival tickets from up there."

Epilogue

W hat has this "crazy idea" of performing a festival of Shakespearean plays in a tent in a small Ontario city accomplished? What has the fulfillment of this mad dream meant to Stratford, to Canada, to theatre, and not least of all, to me?

From a straight commercial or business point of view, between 1953 and 1986 there have been 9,200 performances of 247 productions (excluding musical concerts, workshops, readings, and so on.) By mid-February 1987, box-office receipts totalled over a hundred million dollars. The tourist industry is largely agreed that for every dollar spent at the box office, $5.50 is spent on food, lodging, and other expenses. By this calculation, five hundred and fifty million dollars have been distributed among the twenty-five thousand souls who live in Stratford, Ontario, over a thirty-four-year period. And this income really has been distributed throughout Stratford. For instance, approximately a hundred thousand Festival guests each year stay in commercial accommodation and about half as many in private homes, for a total revenue of some five million dollars each season.

On average, five hundred people are employed year round by the Festival, and at the height of the season, the staff nearly doubles to just under a thousand, including actors, with a total payroll of almost eight and a half million dollars – most of which stays in the city.

The hotel accommodation has also grown. From the eighty-odd hotels rooms in 1953 – some equipped with ropes rolled

up in the corner by the window to be used as fire escapes –
there were 517 in 1986, and this is steadily increasing by
several units every year. Hotels and motels have also been
built for Stratford Festival patrons in St. Mary's, New Ham-
burg, Kitchener, and other nearby towns and cities.

Similarly, the restaurant situation has improved tremen-
dously. From the two typical main-street, small-town eater-
ies in 1953, there are now twenty-one restaurants and cafés,
some of which have received rave reviews in *Gourmet Magazine*
and New York's *Town and Country*.

These figures prove only the financial value of the Festival
to the city of Stratford. Its most important contribution,
however, has been to the development of theatre and other
cultural activities in Canada.

Most immediately, this can be seen in Stratford itself. As
a result of exposure to the standard of artistic activity in
the city, several of our young people, once destined to become
clerks in local stores, have instead become world stars.
Notable among this group was John Boyden, and his story
is worth telling.

In 1953, Boyden was in his teens and was the leading singer
in the local choir at St. John's Church. Guthrie wanted a
boys' choir to sing during the coronation of King Richard
III, and he used a number of the children of St. John's,
including John.

Two years later, the famed German soprano Elisabeth
Schwarzkopf came to Stratford, not only to sing, but to give
master classes. We presented three scholarships to those
classes as a public-relations gesture. One of the winners was
the young Boyden. Toward the end of Schwarzkopf's visit,
she gave a press conference, at which George Kidd, the music
critic, asked if there were any "very promising students?"
Schwarzkopf replied, "Yes; there is one – John Boyden."

After the press conference, I asked the singer if she truly
meant that. "Without doubt," she told me, "he could be one
of the great *lieder* singers in the world." I informed her that
the boy had no money; his mother was a widow, who ran
a little fish and chips shop in town. Not only that, but the
teenager had cancer, and possibly would live only a few more
years.

I went around to local residents and raised $3,000 toward the cost of sending John to England for further training. Not once did anyone suggest that there was no point to the exercise; that he would die soon, anyway.

Boyden went off to England with Schwarzkopf, and studied with the soprano and her voice coach. It was not long before Boyden was known across Europe as Schwarzkopf's young, brilliant protégé. Within six months of his arrival, he sang at Albert Hall; within one year, he performed at Salzburg. When the Lincoln Center opened, Boyden was invited to sing at the debut of its Concert Hall. One of the reviews, I believe it was in *The New York Times*, declared that "if angels sing the way we heard John Boyden sing last night, we should have no fear of dying."

Meanwhile, the top doctors at the Mayo Clinic, as well as others in England and continental Europe, worked with Boyden and exchanged their files regularly. For a long time, he accepted only those engagements that were a short distance from his doctors. He grew steadily weaker, and, eventually, his superb voice was affected. But he lived long enough to assist Robin Phillips's Stratford Choir, helping from a wheelchair and moving the audience to tears. He died shortly after. But had there been no Festival, none of his remarkable career would have occurred.

There were other similar, if less spectacular examples. Barbara Collier, who now sings with European opera companies, and who has returned to sing at the Stratford Festival, is one more. There are too many stories to relate. It's enough to say that many, many people in the theatrical trades across Canada, the United States, and around the world gained immeasurably at Stratford.

Under Mrs. Lois Burdett, a teacher in Hamlet School in our city, a group of fifth- and sixth-graders recently formed their own Shakespearean company, writing and performing their own versions of the Bard's plays. They were invited in April 1986 to help celebrate the sesquicentennial of the State of Texas, and their performance was covered by both the CBC national news and CNN cable news in the U.S.A., England, and Japan.

The success of the Festival has encouraged the development of theatre on a national and international basis. Toronto, which had but two professional theatre companies playing intermittently in the early 1950s – the New Play Society and the Jupiter Theatre – now has over two dozen year-round companies. Admittedly, some of them are still struggling, but Lord knows, that is the nature of the beast!

On a wider scale, it is a little known fact that the Stratford Festival was, to my knowledge, the first major theatre built in North America in this century – and again, because of its success, it started a trend. For the following two decades, hardly a year went by without another theatre being initiated: the O'Keefe Centre in Toronto; the Vancouver Playhouse; the Charlottetown Festival; Les Place des Arts in Montreal. Even in the United States, many theatres can trace their influence back to the Stratford Festival – the Guthrie Theater in Minneapolis, is the prime example, of course. But theatres in Dallas, Los Angeles, Atlanta, and the National Center in Washington, D.C., were all built during this theatrical renaissance. And how many people know that the Rockefeller Foundation sent Jo Mielziner, Elia Kazan, and Robert Whitehead up to Stratford, where they took measurements of the stage and studied seat angles for the Beaumont Theater of the Lincoln Center?

Most North American theatres were less directly influenced than were the Guthrie Theater in Minneapolis and the Lincoln Center. But during the 1960s and 1970s, every few months another sponsor, architect, civic official, would arrive in Stratford to check out "How To Do It."

The Festival has also influenced the theatre world internationally. New theatres in Nottingham, Chichester, and Manchester in England were modelled on Tanya's inspired design. Even the transformation of the Tchaikovski Concert Hall in Moscow into a theatre can be traced to a two-week visit of Nicholai Oklopkov, the Guthrie of the Russian theatre, to Stratford in 1959.

While the Festival has affected many lives in varying degrees, it has probably affected mine most – a proof of the deep importance of cultural activity in all phases of our lives. Solely as a result of the Stratford Festival, I have had the honour – and thrill – of being invited (not for social reasons alone) to Government House in Ottawa, the White House, Buckingham Palace, Government House in Trinidad, even to the Kremlin.

Many times I have been honoured for my work in starting the Shakespeare Festival. In 1967, I was surprised and delighted to be made one of the first Officers of the Order of Canada. Just ten years later, in 1977, the citizens of Stratford named the island in the Avon River, just below the theatre, the Tom Patterson Island. I was much amused to be able to prove John Donne wrong about no man being an island.

With all its problems, setbacks, even heartbreaks, the Stratford Festival has helped create for me a marvellous and most exciting life in the arts. And I like to think that, given the right times and circumstances, and with the co-operation of enthusiastic people, what happened at Stratford, Ontario, in 1952, 1953, and beyond, is proof that any such dream, if desired strongly enough, can eventually come true.